DEATH of the

ORG CHART

Rise of the Organizational Graph

An introduction to The Organizational Cognizance® Model and the Organizational Graph©.

WALT BROWN

© Walt Brown 2020

Print Hardback ISBN 978-1-7341757-0-7

Print Paperback ISBN 978-1-7341757-5-2

eBook ISBN 978-1-09831-930-4

Testimonials

"If organizational charts could talk, this would be the language they would use. Brown has done a masterful job of capturing the actual complexity of 21st century organizations and boiling it down into a straightforward nomenclature we can all understand and get our heads and hearts around. Then he adds Ograph as a software solution to capture, document and visualize the work, this language. Winner, winner. James P. - CEO 14,000 person Research Organization."

"When you hear Walt talk about Death, (That is what hip insiders shorten the approach to.) you will hear him describe the two questions this approach is in place to answer. From one perspective a CEO can look out and get the answer to: "Who is doing what and why?" and from the opposite perspective an individual can look in and get the answer to: "What am I doing and why?" What is really neat is this, he is not reinventing the wheel, he is taking the wheel we are familiar with, the Org Chart, and giving it real-world, deeper meaning. Worth the read and the investment to make it happen in your company." JC and PM – Co-CEOs 48 Location Franchisee

"The most unexpected reward was how empowering this approach has been for our people. How quickly they bought in was a huge bonus, almost effortless 10 minutes in. The flower power facilitations were straight forward, people picked it up and then readily filled out the Roles and Job forms. The team approach spurred healthy debate and our work product is strong. We have documentation at a fine level, from the frontlines where the work is really happening. Powerful for the company and powerful for our people. What you can get done in a half day with this framework that motivates people is nothing short of amazing." Betsy R – CEO Clinical Research Organization

"When I sat down, faced the reality, and modeled the cost to my company of not bringing new people up to speed using the 14 Point Checklist, I saw it was in the hundreds of thousands. We took the plunge and now have a repeatable simple way to keep our on-boarding and training "welcome mat" up to date and ready for the next team member." Clay G - CEO Distribution

"The different ways to visualize the same thing is really strong, sometimes I would look at what we created via a Hierarchical view and it was just scrambled eggs, then I clicked on Symmetrical View, and think, ah ha there it is, then we drill down with the Marquee Zoom tool and it just becomes clear, the software works." Sara H - School Operations Officer

"The really cool thing about using the 14 Point Checklist and the facilitations was it got all of our people into the game. Once our Individual Contributors saw how this was something we were doing "For Them" instead of "To Them", they bought in and the Org Graph bloomed with amazing detail - all supplied by the people who really know what's going on, incredible." Bryan B, CEO Manufacturing

"Our engagement is up, our teams are more effective, people are able to go directly to the right person for an answer, when we want to change something, like a process, we can *SEE* via the software who it will impact and get them involved. All of this was hidden in the past behind layers of folders and files, text and outlines, never in simple diagrams and pictures, very powerful." David H, – CEO Financial Services

As an international marketing and manufacturing company doing over $400 million a year in sales, we were in desperate need of a way to capture and document the Core Processes our business was leaning on. We had outgrown the tribal knowledge and our NetSuite implementation was floundering. OGOG, OGraph and the OGraph BPM module brought it all together. Now when we sit down with an employee to describe what they are accountable and responsible for it is crystal clear. When we process an issue, we can go straight to the source. It is either an unclear Role definition or an unclear Process issue. Ryan G - CEO

Dedication

For the Individual Contributors who labor under the yoke of organizational confusion and dysfunction.

Acknowledgments

Special thanks to the thinkers, leaders and teams of hundreds of companies who have participated in this journey of awareness and Cognizance.

About the author

Since 2007, Walt has identified as a focused, full-time Implementer of the Entrepreneurial Operating System (EOS). He was the fourth EOSi in the system and has had the honor of guiding more than 180 companies through the process to graduation. Today, he is still an active EOSi but is circling in some extended orbits as the creator of the Organizational Cognizance® Model, the "Christopher Columbus" of the Organizational Graph™, co-founder of 7Q7P™ with Allen Cobb, and, via a 10x collaboration with Brendan Madden, is co-creator of a sophisticated Organizational Graph software solution that you can find at https://ograph.io and learn about at https://organizationalcognizance.university

Working exclusively with senior leadership teams and since 2006, Walt has averaged more than 130 days a year sequestered in session rooms, facilitating the gutsy work of working on one's business. His work focuses on diving deep with companies and non-profits, helping them create accuracy and awareness around who is doing what, why, and how. From this deep work rose the solution of what we call the Organizational Cognizance Model, and the 14 Point Checklist, leading to the manifestation of an Organizational Graph.

He started his work-life as an accounting and statistics guy with the CPA firm now called E&Y. He then founded four companies, selling all four in 2006 after twenty years at the helm, leaving that orbit and moving to his coaching and facilitation orbit.

Walt is based in the Research Triangle area of North Carolina, where he lives with his wife of 35 years, Anne, an attorney by profession, who raised two daughters, Jane and Marion, with very little meaningful help from Walt. Jane was a Chemical and Biological Engineering undergrad and master's graduate student at Princeton now at Booz Allen Hamilton. Marion is an honors UNC Chapel Hill Law School grad, publishing articles around the SEC and block-chain currency, she is with Moore & Van Allen in Charlotte NC. Marion majored in Economics, Honors English, and Studio Art. Yes, Walt loves his family and is very proud of them.

In 2015 Walt formalized the 7 Questions and 7 Promises Framework for building organizational engagement and culture and authored *The Patient Organization,* published by ForbesBooks in 2017.

He enjoys honoring his faith, time with family, mountain biking, sailboat racing, powder skiing in Alta, coaching youth football, walking beaver dams, and duck hunting, but, mostly removing the yoke of organizational confusion and dysfunction from the neck of individual contributors by training Coaches Organizational Cognizance® University and pressing Ograph.io into the world.

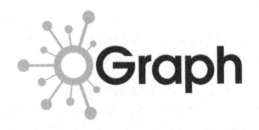

TABLE OF CONTENTS

The 14 Point Checklist

What if everyone could answer these 14 things about their Job, in detail, without hesitation?

- What is the Purpose of my Job?
- What Roles do I fill as part of my Job? What is the Purpose of each Role?
- Who do I report to?
- Who is my Mentor?
- Who do I turn to for Coaching in each of my Roles?
- What Teams am I part of?
- What Meetings will I attend?
- What Entities (clients, projects, contracts, etc.) will I interact with?
- What Process do I participate in?
- What Procedures/Work Inst./Policies will I follow?
- What Systems do I interface with and need to master?
- What are my Objectives?
- What are my Key Results?
- What Skills or Competencies do I need now and in the future?

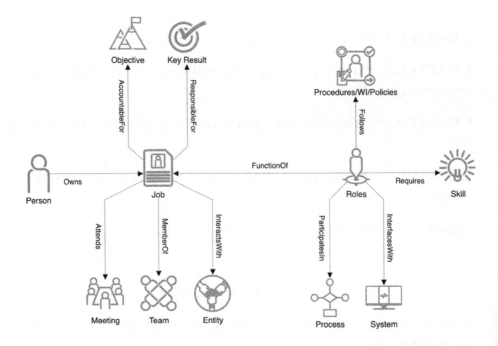

One Example of the Basic Organizational Cognizance® Model Graph Database Schema

CHAPTER 1

THE CASE FOR ORGANIZATIONAL COGNIZANCE

Rumor has it that when business guru Peter Drucker was on his deathbed, someone asked him, what is the most important question in business? He supposedly replied, "Who is doing what?"

Such a simple question and yet it has never been more difficult to answer. Obviously, this query implies others. Even in Drucker's time, it could have been expanded to: "Who is doing what, with whom, for whom, how, and why?" These days, we must also add, "…using what software, on what platforms, as part of what teams, through what communication channels, after which meetings…" ad infinitum.

> Modern day business guru Dan Sullivan of Strategic Coach™ teaches entrepreneurs that the key to their time freedom and ultimate success is to think **Who not How** first. He couples this thinking with a tool he calls his Impact Filter that gives the Who a well thought out reason that the Who can intellectually and emotionally buy in to and figure out how to do it. The Who, in our model is the Individual Contributor (IC) who is moved toward cognizance via Sullivan's Impact Filter which basically outlines the Purpose of the Role the IC is getting ready to take on.

The old question, like the classic Organizational Chart, gets to something vital, but in a way that misses the ever more complicated reality of 21st century organizations. Not only has "Who is doing what?" turned into an incredibly complex question, "What am I doing and why?" has become a painfully difficult one for workers to answer.

Our goal here is to provide an approach and a set of tools that allow both leaders and Individual Contributors (ICs) to answer these extended Drucker questions honestly and completely. Our aim is fourfold:

- To help people understand organizational complexity – the messy complicated reality, not the neat simplicity portrayed in Org Charts. CEOs will be able to get the answer to "Who is doing what, and why?" and individual contributors will be able to get their answers to "What am I doing, and why?"
- To provide a clear foundation for working within this complexity by supplementing your thinking with a 21^{s}century Organizational Cognizance® Model.
- Introduce a software approach to augment your 2-D Org Chart with a dynamic, interactive 3-D Organizational Graph that allows one to capture and visualize the complex.
- Finally, to provide thinking tools and facilitation examples that help organizations get buy-in, build clarity, transparency, and, ultimately, "Organizational Cognizance" into their companies.

What is Organizational Cognizance?

Organizational Cognizance is about building awareness and knowledge for Individual Contributors and helping them, their fellow team members, and leaders to understand precisely how they are connected to others and to the organization at a fine level, where they fit and how they belong.

If we had to write an equation for Organizational Cognizance, it might read:

Awareness + Knowledge + Connectivity = Organizational Cognizance

Perspective: The Individual Contributor. A quick example will make the concept clear. Imagine yourself as a new employee, or Individual Contributor, starting at an organization, and you are presented with the company's Organizational Graph, based on the Organizational Cognizance Model. The Model is built around your Job and the Roles you hold in that Job. Individual Contributors wear various hats, and most Jobs include at least several Roles, as we'll explore in depth in Chapter 2. A Job called "Sales Associate," for example, might include a Customer Greeter Role, a

Sales Consultant Role, a Sales Invoicing Role, a Market Feedback Role, and a Business Networking Role.

On day one, the Organizational Cognizance Model provides you as an individual contributor with the answers to all of these 14 questions; the 14 Point Checklist:

- What is the Purpose of my Job?
- What Roles do I fill as part of my Job? What is the Purpose of each Role?
- Who do I report to?
- Who is my Mentor?
- Who do I turn to for Coaching in each of my Roles?
- What Teams am I part of?
- What Meetings will I attend?
- What Entities (clients, projects, contracts, etc.) will I interact with?
- What Processes do I participate in?
- What Procedures/Work Inst./Policies will I follow?
- What Systems do I interface with and need to master?
- What are my Objectives?
- What are my Key Results?
- What Skills or Competencies do I need now and in the future?

We are not suggesting that an IC can be Organizationally Cognizant an hour after filling out HR's forms, yet, armed with all of this info, a team member can be pretty damn aware on Day One. She will understand where and how she fits in, to a degree that some employees never enjoy, even after years at an organization. She immediately has a map to reference, independently, and already is travelling down the road to feeling that she believes and belongs and understands her Accountabilities. She is starting off with the answers she needs to become Organizationally Cognizant.

We used the word "awareness" above and it's certainly related, but we want to emphasize that the state we are describing as Organizational Cognizance for our hypothetical team member is much deeper than mere awareness. A couple of examples will help.

Let's say a company occupies five floors of a skyscraper. ICs show up to various departments on five contiguous levels every day from nine to five. Proximity breeds *awareness* for these employees – they know where Accounts Receivable is, three floors down, and that a dozen or so people work in Marketing two floors up, but they don't have Cognizance. They don't comprehend at a deep level what's going on outside of their cubicle, and certainly not outside of their department. They don't understand how their work affects other Teams and Processes, what the Purpose of every piece of their Job is or how each tie to the Purpose or Objectives of their Team, Department, Organization. They are not Cognizant.

Humans share the same five senses. Touching, smelling, seeing, hearing, or tasting something means that you are *aware* of it. What's that I smell? Smoke. Smelling smoke is awareness but comprehending that the smoke you smell is wood smoke from a cozy fireplace versus an electrical fire starting on the floor below you is Cognizance. The latter level of comprehension requires grasping a bigger picture, understanding context, getting how things are connected, what they mean, and where you fit.

Cognizance is easy when it's just you. We often use the example of Paul's Painting Company, a one-man business. When we list out all the things that have to be done and thought about for this tiny organization to function, the list runs into the hundreds. There are five *thinking* Roles (as we said, we break Jobs down into Roles in the Organizational Cognizance Model) and dozens upon dozens of *doing* Roles. This level of complexity exists for a tiny contractor that doesn't even use a computer, and Paul has Cognizance because it's just him. He occupies every Role, so he understands on a deep level how they relate and what their Purposes are as they align with the whole. Once you begin adding people, even a handful, it becomes much harder to achieve Cognizance or to answer: "Who is doing what and why?"

COGNIZANCE BREEDS ACCOUNTABILITY

Since selling my company Layline.com in 2006, I have been stacking days on top of Malcom Gladwell's 10,000+ hours, helping more than 200 organizations large and small, in many fields, build Organizational Cognizance by figuring out *who is doing what, with whom, for whom, how, and why?* This work led me to the Seven Questions and Seven Promises critical to cultivating culture and engaged team members, detailed in my book, *The Patient Organization.* (Engaged ICs answer "yes" to these 7 Questions: *Do I belong? Do I believe? Am I Accountable? Am I measured well? Am I heard? Am I developed? Do I have balance?*). The book you're reading grew out of that earlier one as I began to focus on the tricky "hinge" question of the Seven, *Am I Accountable?*

True Accountability goes hand in glove with what I began to think of as "Organizational Cognizance," a term that crystallized a lifetime of work, starting, running, and, ultimately, coaching companies. We know from experience that people generally want to do a good job. They want Accountability, but organizational life has grown so complex and opaque that they are hazy on their Roles and Purpose, how the many pieces connect, and where they fit. Most organizations don't offer them true Accountability, and the skeletal old Org Chart doesn't really help.

What if we could radically clarify Accountability? Imagine an organization where Individual Contributors are truly Cognizant of the Process and Procedures/Work Instructions/Policies they touch and the Systems they **InterfaceWith**. Imagine an organization where every IC fully appreciates why each Meeting they attend is important, how it relates to their Roles and Purpose. Imagine the individual who only knows they must pull Lever Y in order to collect a check, suddenly comprehending how this work impacts the work of colleagues, clients, and the organization as a whole. Imagine an organization where all systems we log into – ERP, HRIS, accounting, manufacturing, quality control, etc. – are fully mapped to Jobs, Roles and Objectives, integrated, with connections clearly spelled out.

An organization with this sort of transparency and clarity creates incredible levels of engagement and belief. What do we mean by *belief*? *As anyone who has worked with me or read The Patient Organization knows, we firmly believe that an organization is a fiction, only given meaning and power by those who believe in it. If you have 200 people and 90 believe the organization means one thing, and 110 believe something else, you have two organizations, not one. You have already been divided and are on your way to being conquered.* If some ICs don't believe at all, the organization suffers. If enough stop believing, it disappears.

It's tough to believe in something – Jesus, Buddha, a country, a company – if you don't have a true sense of what it is and how you're connected to it. Belief, at the risk of stating the obvious, demands Cognizance.

THE ORGANIZATIONAL COGNIZANCE MODEL AND THE ORGANIZATIONAL GRAPH

That all sounds good, we can hear some readers saying, but it's too complicated *man*, especially for a new employee. Yes, if you're relying on a traditional 2-D Org Chart, it's far too complex, which is why we developed the Organizational Cognizance Model Graph Schema, a "3-D" visualization that makes all of the "Nodes" listed in the questions above (Job, Roles, Teams, Meetings, Processes, Systems, etc.) and the IC's relationship to them crystal clear (more on Nodes and Relationships / Connections / Edges later). We have also built user-friendly Organizational Graph software that allows ICs and leaders to quickly and easily build out, view, and investigate their own Organizational Cognizance Models. It is now "easy" to adjust existing Models and to gain insight with a variety of dynamic views (hierarchical, circular, symmetrical, global, orthogonal, etc.). We call this software solution an Organizational Graph, https://ograph.io.

The icons, which represent Nodes in the Organizational Graph, and the "Edges" – those lines / arrows indicating how things connect – can be manipulated with a few mouse clicks in the Organizational Graph software, then expanded, and viewed through various filters and lenses to build Organizational Cognizance for the IC or leadership. Details and Rich Text get built into each node, where you can upload files, embed videos, pictures, files, create links etc. for a colorful universe of information – easily accessed, expanded, or contracted with a click.

This intuitive software is eminently helpful, but certainly not a requirement for developing Organizational Cognizance. The important thing is finding a friendly, manageable way to visualize all relevant Nodes – Roles, Meetings, Procedures/Work Instructions/Policies, Processes, etc. – and how they connect. Spreadsheets and other tools can also be enlisted. I was personally thrilled to discover the potential of Graph Database technology (think use cases like Facebook and LinkedIn, graph software like Neo4J, Amazon's Neptune, Microsoft Graph, etc.) used in this software for two reasons: first, because it makes visualization so easy and functional, and _second, because technology has played such a large role in complicating organizational life, we figured it was high time that a tech solution made our structures more navigable._

Think of the layers upon layers of complexity that have been added to organizations – and on the backs of ICs over the years – many of them a result of advancing technologies. Once upon a time, employees at Organization X worked at a central location. They reported to a single boss from a relatively static Job. Communication was spoken – face-to-face or on the phone – and each process tended to have a person attached to it (a paper invoice arrived in an envelope, and a person opened it; he put it in a box for the person who approved it; she stamped it and moved it into another box for the person who made manual journal entries into a ledger…).

The old formula was **Job = Role = Person**, 1:1:1. Hierarchies were rigid, and, as on sailing ships of old, _thinking_ was done mostly at the very top – by a captain and a tiny handful of lieutenants. The handwork was done by sailors actually grabbing hold of and muscling the lines. In that paper-based world, the two-dimensional Org Chart provided an adequate birds-eye view for a top-down "command-and-control" model.

Today, there's no more central 9-to-5 location. ICs are working remotely, from home, at co-working spaces, on trains, and in coffee shops – according to all sorts of flexible schedules. They often don't know when reaching out if a colleague is across town or across the globe. The office is defined by cell phones, laptops, tablets, and WiFi – not a desk, landline, calculator, four walls and a window. An IC reports to various people, depending on the project, task, or team on deck, though, practically speaking, she might have no traditional "boss" or "supervisor" on a daily basis.

And we haven't yet mentioned the number of systems, automated processes, and communication channels that even a frontline IC now encounters on a daily basis. In my work with organizations of all types and sizes, we sometimes ask leaders to take an inventory of the various systems that their ICs use to communicate. A thorough list often includes twenty or more. Add to this CRM (customer relationship management) software, vendor platforms, human resources systems, facilities apps, internal networks, and the countless other systems and processes now present at a typical organization, and it's no mystery why "Who is doing what?" looks more like the scary lid to Pandora's box than a simple question.

We have a client that calls their many systems their "list of Slogins," as in, all the stuff you have to log into and slog through

These systems, apps, processes, and communication channels are usually introduced by well-meaning decision makers to improve service or efficiency, to save labor, or make life easier in some way. Many do. Many are invaluable tools, but all add a layer of complexity. Like meetings and memos, they proliferate insidiously until an Individual Contributor who wants to figure out her Roles and Purpose and how they relate to long-term Objectives might as well be delving into astrophysics. Simply trying to understand why a particular Meeting matters or who to turn to for Coaching on X or Y can be a daunting prospect. So, what does the IC do? Nothing. They adopt the attitude that it's better to keep one's mouth shut and appear uninformed rather than opening it and removing all doubt. Let's break this fear cycle.

COMPLEXITY TESTS HUMAN LIMITS

Into this environment steps a well-meaning leader who announces, we're going to begin using Slack – or Asana or Monday.com or some other platform designed to help the flow of work and communication – and the IC's heart sinks. The new app or platform might be great, but, the IC thinks, it is one more system to interface with, and we haven't even come close to understanding the existing Systems, Meetings, Procedures/Work Inst./Policies, Reporting, Workflow, etc. or how I fit into this puzzle. It's as if they have been captured by the Borg, aliens in *Star Trek* who coopt all technologies they encounter and turn individual beings into drones through a process called "assimilation." "We are BORG (short for cyborg) you will be assimilated"

> **Complexity and Invisible Processes** – With the digitization and automation of so much work, the actual flow of work is hard for ICs to see or even imagine, these Processes/workflows have become hidden from view more and more as we link this system to that system. However, this does not mean the IC is excluded, and an understanding of what, when and where one participates in a Workflow is more important than ever to improve and refine an organization.

Without Organizational Cognizance, any new System – and we are not knocking the random examples above – feels like a fancy to-do list, yet another box to check, another Slogin. We share the following formula and accompanying graphic with my clients to illustrate my point about creeping complexity in organizations.

The first time we saw this arrows diagram describing complexity was in 2007 when Gino Wickman drew it on a whiteboard to describe his first "Leadership Ability," the Ability to Simplify.

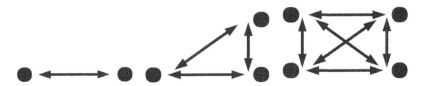

Of course, my sick statistics mind goes into formula creation mode and I think: N, or the number of "Nodes" (interacting entities) squared, minus the number of Nodes equals C, or the level of Complexity.

So, for instance, if there are only two Nodes and two directions for interaction (represented by two arrow tips in the illustration above), the level of Complexity is just two ($2^2 - 2 = 2$). As you can see from our graphic, adding one Node, for a total of just three, triples the level of Complexity (from two arrow tips to six), and going from four nodes to five, raises the Complexity level from twelve to twenty.

$$N^2 - N = C$$

Research shows that the number of variables humans can mentally handle while trying to solve a problem – whether that's baking a pie or closing a sale – is three. In their article "How Many Variables Can Humans Process?" published in the journal *Psychological Science,* Graeme S. Halford and his coauthors found that juggling four elements is very difficult for people, five nearly impossible.

So, yes, adding that new app, System, mandatory Meeting, etc., however benign the intention, is a big deal. Interestingly, the researchers behind the *Psychological Science* article found that the subjects in their experiments naturally tried to group like variables, to establish connections, and to break complexity down into navigable chunks. Job titles are an easy example of this – tons of complexity gets shoved into one Pandora's Box, represented as a word or two on an Org Chart… You get the picture and why the old Org Chart, with its Pandora's boxes, is going the way of the dinosaur. Humans crave understanding. They want to know where they fit and the ways in which their Nodes, however they're defined for a given challenge or organization, relate. They want Organizational Cognizance.

THE ORG CHART –

A 2-D TOOL IN A 3-D WORLD

Not only do ICs want Organizational Cognizance, the conscientious ones are continually striving for it in their heads, attempting to make sense of all the Meetings, Mentors, Systems, Processes, Projects, Teams, etc. with little more to go on than a 2-D Org Chart, a top-down, hierarchical tool that hasn't changed in thousands of years, (remember the Terracotta Warriors buried with a Chinese emperor circa 210 B.C.). It is closely tied to its military roots, soldiers ordered by "rank and file." Today's ICs still hear echoes of the old MO: "Why?! Because I said so! Now, get back in line!"

Are architects and engineers still using pencils? Of course not. With the help of Computer-Aided Design, they engage in incredible 3-D modelling and produce designs that would have been impossible thirty years ago. Engineers can now build entire machines with 3-D printers, and medical diagnosis has leaped forward with MRI imaging that can distinguish types of tissue at a fine level and present their complex gradations with dazzlingly clear 3-D visualizations.

Only in business are we still relying on a 2-D, the-world-is-flat analogue tool, the old-fashioned Org Chart, to understand a complex, technologically advanced environment. It's as if NASA or SpaceX were relying on cave drawings to run their space programs.

The resulting lack of clarity for those conscientious ICs, the stars who organizations should be nurturing, manifests as frustration and, ultimately, disengagement. More than two-thirds of U.S. workers are not actively engaged at work, according to Gallup's famous engagement survey, and over years of working with organizations of all types and sizes, we have realized that the absence of Organizational Cognizance is often to blame.

Poor engagement, of course, hits the bottom-line in all sorts of ways – performance, retention, sick time…If, for example, your average retention period is 3.2 years, essentially, 30 percent of your ICs will be new every year. How long does it take to reach maximum ROI (return on investment) with these new hires? My clients tell me that before they installed an Organizational Cognizance approach, their people would spend three to four months just getting "up to speed" – understanding what they should be doing, who to turn to with questions, where the nondairy creamer is stored. This is time when they're not really earning or producing for the firm. In year two they reach 50 percent ROI, and at year three they get to 75 percent. It is only in year four that they can count on 100 percent capacity ROI.

Imagine if you could shorten the hemorrhaging period and get ICs up to speed in two months, to 75 percent effective in twelve months, and to 100 percent by the end of year two. Assuming your retention stays at 3.2 years, (and, by the way, it won't with Organizational Cognizance – it will improve to four and five years) you will enjoy a permanent 15 percent gain in employee productivity. That's FIFTEEN PERCENT straight to your EBITDA.

The obvious problem here is that ICs are moving on after year three, you are continually retraining, and the organization never sees a decent ROI. At Layline, a pre-Internet catalog business I started many years ago that became a pretty successful dot-com, during orientation we always had a second-year Coach immediately teach every new crew member how to navigate MOM (our product and order system) and DAD (our searchable tribal knowledge intranet).

When someone asked a question at Layline, we could lovingly say, "Have you checked with MOM or DAD? I think they have the answer." With this approach and backbone in place, people got up to speed very quickly. This solid frame of self-serve reference helped them understand our Systems, Procedures/Work Inst./Policies, Workflow, Meetings, etc. – and they learned to find the answers to most questions on their own. If MOM and DAD didn't have an answer, we discussed what it should be, and with guidance from his or her Coach, the *answer-seeker* would do the update. Like the Organizational Cognizance Model, which draws heavily from this experience, it was a self-maintaining, self-improving system updated by ICs, the real-world users.

Yes, we are in essence reproducing the MOM / DAD solution, but maybe it is called a LMS, learning management system, to use fancy words.

The key point, as we'll explore in depth later, is that my clients take the same systematic approach to keeping their Organizational Cognizance Models up-to-date. The people interfacing with the Nodes and Connections data are the ones who update it and improve it. It is a dispersed effort, owned by the ICs who are using it every day. *If you can't buy this, then you are a dinosaur and should stop reading now, but, wait, dinosaurs don't read, right?*

Imagine how much time organizations following the Organizational Cognizance Model, with Jobs defined by Roles clearly mapped to all relevant Nodes, can save on training and on-boarding. (Yes, the Organizational Cognizance software can double as your LMS, or Learning Management System, which, in essence, is what it functions as. Whether the training material is embedded in the Skill Node as Rich Text, attachments, or videos, or you use the Skill Node to link to your existing LMS, it will be easy to navigate from one central location, tied to one's Role, with home plate as the Person – our primary Node.) How much money and effort might be saved if you could cut in half the time it took to get a new IC to the status of Minimum Viable Employee, to 75 percent effective, or to 100 percent ROI? How might organizational performance improve if by reducing frustration and boosting engagement, the OC Model lengthened your average retention time from 3.2 years to four or five?

TAKE THE RED PILL!

Skeptics can be forgiven at this point for wondering if in promoting the Org Graph and Organizational Cognizance Model, we are guilty of the same sort of complexity creep we criticized earlier. Isn't this, like other flashy apps, just an additional box to check or hoop to jump through, yet another Node making things more complicated for ICs?

Our sincere answer is, no, absolutely not. Organizational Cognizance is about visualizing and understanding what's already there, "the messy reality" of your organization, as we said at the start of this chapter. The Org Graph and Organizational Cognizance Model don't add anything new. They simply provide tools that allow ICs to fully understand their existing Roles and Purpose, the Meetings they already attend, the Systems they already interface with, the Processes they already participate in. OC doesn't add complexity, it reduces it by bringing clarity and transparency.

A business guide and computer science friend of mine, Brent Sprinkle, argues, *"... software is something you use to automate what you're already doing and have already mastered versus forcing you to do something you're not already doing and have not mastered."* You can think of the Org Graph and Organizational Cognizance Model, then, as automating and elucidating a process that's already taking place in the brains of frustrated, confused, and often overwhelmed ICs. The Org Graph simply helps them to connect the dots, to visualize the connections and Nodes they are already a part of and interacting with, but are not yet fully Cognizant of.

At a critical juncture in the film, *The Matrix,* the maverick Morpheus offers the confused main character, Neo, a choice:

> "This is your last chance. After this, there is no turning back. You take the blue pill—the story ends, you wake up in your bed and believe whatever you want to believe. You take the red pill, you stay in Wonderland, and *I show you how deep the rabbit hole goes.* Remember: all I'm offering is the *truth.*"

The Organizational Cognizance Model and Org Graph simply offer a way to visualize the truth about 21st-century organizations, with all their Systems, Procedures/Work Inst./Policies, Teams, Meetings, Processes, etc. If, as we have argued, an organization is a fiction resting on the belief of its ICs, handing out Blue Pills and the message "believe whatever you want to believe" is beyond risky. Instead of one organization built on a set of shared beliefs (the Red Pill), in the Blue Pill scenario, you sleep and wind up with as many organizations as you have employees, none of them aligning with the actual mission and Purpose.

Clarity point, no, we are not completely throwing out the Org Chart, that would be like throwing the baby out with the bathwater. The baby, your Org Chart, just needs to grow, learn, become self-aware, self-feeding as it grows to adulthood and cognizance as an Org Graph.

In *The Matrix,* Neo doesn't just feel that there is an entire world hidden beneath the surface, one he glimpses but can't grasp, he is desperate to unlock its mysteries. He wants to understand. He wants Cognizance. So do your ICs. Give it to them. Pop the Red Pill with me in Chapter 2 as we delve deeper into the Organizational Cognizance Model.

CHAPTER 2

EXPLORING THE ORGANIZATIONAL COGNIZANCE MODEL AND ORG GRAPH

In this chapter, we'll explore the Organizational Cognizance Model and the Org Graph in greater depth, demonstrating how a focus on Roles, Purpose, Nodes, and Edges can bring clarity to an organization and Cognizance to its ICs. First, though, I want to relate an experience I recently had during a two-day strategic retreat I was facilitating for a client. If your organization is anything like the 1,000s we have graduated from the EOS® program, this short anecdote demonstrates the kind of frustration that's simmering in your ranks and why the classic Org Chart can't address it.

The client in question is a janitorial supply distributor, which is why the owner's 5:30 a.m. F3 workout group has nicknamed him "Two-Ply." The company is sizeable – more than $100 million in annual sales – and cute names aside, no laughing matter. I'd been coaching leaders at this organization for two years, and pretty much from day one, we realized that the Director of Sales, who'd been with the company for thirty years, simply didn't get it. We worked with him, giving him the chance to really define the Roles that comprised his Job and to develop a go-to-market strategy the company could support, but to no avail. Three months before the annual meeting, leadership helped him select retirement, and about a month before this meeting, they brought in a new Sales Director, who we'll call Jack.

The first day of an annual meeting for us is all about team health and getting people to really speak their minds. Senior leaders, including the new Sales Director, Jack, were in attendance, as was one of the organization's top Sales Reps. It's a sales-based business, so we wanted a strong voice from the salesforce present, someone who spends his time in the field.

Near the end of the first day, this experienced Sales Rep, who we'll call Mike, finally blew his top. We had been talking about the organization's Core Values, Purpose, Trust, and Belief – topics I covered in depth in my previous book, *The Patient Organization* – when Mike blurted out that the company "has never had sales leadership." When encouraged to speak his mind, he explained that none of the Sales Reps knew what a new account was defined as, what the marketing strategy was, or what the focus should be. People weren't sure who to report to about what, who should be Coaching them, or what Teams they were a part of. Should a new account be defined as $5,000 in annual sales, $12,000, $20,000? The targets seemed always to be moving. Who was the organization's ideal client, Mike wondered, who should they be going after?

Mike enjoyed talking about Core Values and organizational Purpose, but such discussions seemed futile when he didn't understand his own Purpose, where he fit in this organization, or how its various parts (think "Nodes," though he didn't use that term) were supposed to connect and work together. Not a great way to end the first day, especially for a company that just had its best year ever and should have been celebrating.

The next morning, we came in and did an exercise we call Cracking Eggs and Making Omelets to detail the Job and Roles held by Jack, the new Sales Director. WE will go through this exercise step by step in the next chapter, on facilitation, but for now, suffice it to say, that with input from the team of leaders, we were able to lay out all of Jack's responsibilities and Roles, organized around the company's sales structure. Below are the eight critical parts of his Job, or "Roles," that we came up with (Note: you can add "How we do…" in front of each Role for more clarity. For instance, Jack owned the "How we do Prospecting" Role and the "How we do Closing" Role).

1. Prospecting
2. Closing
3. Client Retention
4. Team Leadership (recruiting, onboarding, engaging, and retaining ICs)
5. Product Inventory / Process
6. Market Feedback (product mix / info)
7. Sales Team Training
8. Overall Sales Direction and Corporate Integration (revenue, margins)

In the interests of space, I'm only presenting the finished framework here. We spent a couple hours building this list, discussing each Role, what it entailed, and how it connected with Individual Contributors in sales. It then became Jack's task, with input from other leaders, to write a Purpose Statement for every one of his Roles and to set long-term and short-term Objectives for each.

When we'd finished the exercise, we turned to Mike, the frustrated Sales Rep, and asked, if Jack actually executes and leads from these Roles, does this fill the sales leadership vacuum? Do you understand now where to go for answers and where direction will come from? Yes, said Mike, looking energized. This is a forty-four-year-old guy with three children, whose frustration had been growing in direct proportion to his desire to excel. Was he relieved? You better believe it. Mike was suddenly engaged, and Jack, a sharp guy and new to the team, understood the many facets of his job on a much deeper level. Both had taken major steps toward Organizational Cognizance.

With input from colleagues and leaders, Mike, like Jack, will need to define his Roles as Sales Rep and build Purpose Statements and Objectives for each (we'll show you step by step in the next chapter how to do this for an entire organization). The Sales Director and the Sales Rep then fill out the Nodes and Edges for every one of their Roles, using the one-page Organizational Cognizance Model Role / Job Capture Template or capturing these in their Org Graph software. We'll explore how Nodes and Edges function in a moment, but first, let's take a closer look at the notion of "Roles," which are the basic building blocks and starting point for the Organizational Cognizance Model.

Almost any Job includes several Roles. From the list in our example above, we observe that the Job of Sales Director, held by Jack, is made up of eight Roles – one called Prospecting, another called Closing, a third called Client Retention, etc. WE hope readers can see straightaway that thinking in terms of Roles and not just Jobs provides everyone at the organization with a clearer and more specific view of what's going on.

WE cannot tell you how many times over the years that WE have encountered new "Marketing Directors" who aren't clear what actual work that amorphous title entails. When, however, we break the "Job" listed on the old Org Chart down into Roles, clarity starts to emerge. The job of Marketing Director often includes these Roles: Marketing Strategy for New Leads, Marketing Strategy for New Hires, Product Positioning, Copy Editor, Art Director, Online Advertising Coordinator, Brand Positioning Cop, Supervisor / Mentor / Coach.

Just by listing the Roles – we haven't even gotten to their attendant Nodes and Edges yet – you can already imagine a set of Skills, Objectives, Responsibilities, Measures, etc. arising from the more specific terms.

"Online Advertising Coordinator" implies that the owner of this Role knows something about search engine optimization, Google AdWords, and a range of Internet ad platforms. Depending on priorities, long-term Objectives might include things like maximizing our website experience or online sales, and Key Results will likely be measured in the short term by page views, click-throughs, monthly online revenue, etc.

The following image often helps ICs and leaders grasp the utility of this new way of thinking about organizational structure. Imagine your Job as a domed-topped table with your Roles as boxes hanging off it. WE tell clients that our goal is to create such clear Jobs and Roles that we have no confusion. An issue shaped like a ball-bearing drops from the sky and lands on our domed Job table. What is it going to do? Roll is the answer, of course, and our goal is to be sure that nothing slips through our box-shaped Roles and hits the floor. Nothing gets stuck between Roles or gets footballed back and forth between them, and we don't ever have a Role that is full and cannot take anything else because then our rolling issue will spill over and hit the floor. Roles are the ultimate catchers and handlers of issues in our organization.

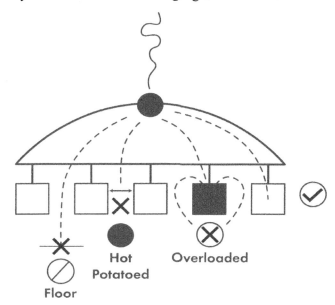

We are not suggesting that the category of "Job" should disappear, only that the term "Role" adds detail and is more precise. Role, which for me was a natural outgrowth of my sports and sailing experience, has the precision we are looking for. Consider the difference between telling someone that their Job is "football player" versus explaining to them their Job is "Special Teams Football Player" and they will play this Role on Kick-offs, this Role on Punt Returns, this Role on Field-goals. Hearing the Roles gives the Individual Contributor a much better sense of expectation, Purpose and orientation. It's the first step in understanding where they fit on the team and how they interact with Teammates, Coaches, and Systems, the first step toward Organizational Cognizance.

HR NOMENCLATURE: Unfortunately, there is no "HR Standards Body" that dictates the nomenclature around HR. Below is a simple table you can reference if the words we are using make your head spin. It includes the vocabulary and perspective, a couple of other examples, and the specific taxonomy used by EOS® (the Entrepreneurial Operating System™), one of today's popular Organizational Operating Systems businesses adopt to help focus and execute their visions.

Model	Org Chart "Box" Name	Sub Unit	Named Descriptor 1	Named Descriptor 2
Org Cognizance® Model	*Job*	*Roles*	*Purpose Statements*	*Accountable / Responsible*
Org Chart Example A	*Job*	*Roles*	*Duties*	-
Org Chart Example B	*Position*	-	*Roles and Resp.*	-
EOS® Accountability Chart™ Model	*Seat*	*Roles*	-	-

Note: We are firm on the term Jobs and the spot they hold because almost 100 percent of the HRIS systems out there – workday.com, paycor.com, ADP.com, NetSuite, Certipay, etc. – tie *Jobs* to their Org Charts. You post *Jobs* to *Job boards*, where people are looking for *Jobs*, which are filled by humans. You get a *Job*, you see yourself in the *Job* box on the Org Chart.

Accounting and Finance use those *Jobs* to create budgets...*Jobs, Jobs, Jobs*. The term isn't going anywhere, so it is ours to use.

"But what about when we have an *open Position*?" you ask, and, what you mean is you have a Job opening in your Org Chart and you are interchanging the word Job and Position, well, randomly. In the nomenclature of OCM, this is a misuse of the word "Position." Our goal is to get very precise in your organizational language, use ONE word to mean ONE thing, not three or four, resulting in no clear meaning.

In the Organizational Cognizance Model, that hole in the Org Chart is an "open Job," not an open Position. This Job, like all Jobs, contains Roles that are explained by Purpose Statements; paragraphs that describe the roles, responsibilities and duties.

FLEXIBLE, DYNAMIC ORGANIZATIONAL GRAPHS

Strategizing around Roles is also more flexible than focusing solely on Jobs. Jobs, like Org Charts, tend to be static. Jack, the new Sales Director at our janitorial supply firm, will probably have that same title, "Job," and slot on the old Org Chart for the duration of his time with the company, unless he takes another Job within the organization. Meanwhile, his Roles might shift substantially. A year from now, for instance, a new Role could be added to his list, and an existing Role, say Sales Team Training, could be turned over to a new Job, Assistant Sales Director. This doesn't necessarily mean that Jack will be removed from all training activities, but everyone at the organization would know that Bob, the new Assistant Sales Director, now owns the Role: Sales Team Training. That's his Role; his *domain and authority*, what he is Responsible and Accountable for. He is in charge of the Objectives related to it and will live and die by the Objectives and Results we achieve through Sales Team Training.

Once the Assistant Sales Director takes over the Role called Sales Team Training, Mike, the Sales Rep in our example, will be able to see this adjustment in the Org Graph, reflecting the new reality. If Mike has a part in Sales Training, or suggestions or complaints about it, etc., he will interact with Bob on those issues, though he still reports to Jack on most fronts. Similarly, to return to the sports parallel, when I play the Role (Position) of Center on offence, I am **CoachedBy** the Role (Position) of Offensive-Line

Coach, and when I'm in my Linebacker Role (Position) on defense, I am **CoachedBy** the Defensive-Back Coach Role.

None of these nuances get captured on the rigid Org Chart, which leaders often think of as presenting a skeletal view of an organization. That's actually a pretty good metaphor. For a quick broad glance at organizational hierarchy – the skeleton beneath the headstone – the old Org Chart is useful, though less and less so, since organizations are less rigidly hierarchical and fixed than they used to be.

Like a model skeleton, the classic Org Chart leaves out the nervous system, circulation, respiration, muscles – the living tissue that allows an organization to function on a daily basis. The Org Chart is like an annual old-school X-ray that doesn't change much year to year. Think of the Org Graph, by comparison, as high-resolution 3-D medical imaging updated in real time. It shows all of the systems, types of tissue, and fine gradations in ways that make the incredibly complicated processes responsible for organizational life digestible.

The continual updating of Roles as opposed to Jobs was front and center for me at Layline, the dot.com I started and ran for twenty years, though I didn't yet have an Org Graph. Our selling cycle was very seasonal, with sales ramping up in mid-March and then slowing to a trickle come fall. We had ICs whose Roles would switch from phone work to vendor relations to copy editing depending on the time of year. Their Jobs and titles would remain the same on any Org Chart, but a dynamic Org Graph, based on Roles, would have reflected those seasonal shifts.

Whether Roles shift because of seasonal / cyclical patterns, team realignment, new business, new client demands, new projects, or other reasons, the Org Graph can create and maintain Cognizance even in rapidly evolving environments where Roles shift on a dime.

Nerd Time: GRAPH DATABASE. AKA: "A Graph"

A simple Graph is made up of Nodes and Edges (aka Connections, Relationships), and each of these Nodes and Edges have Labels and Properties.

	Labels	**Properties**
Nodes (aka Objects)	*Node Label*	*Node Property*
Edges (aka Connections / Relationships)	*Edge Label*	*Edge Property*

Popular Graph Developer Programs include Neo4j, Amazon's Neptune, the Microsoft Graph Engine, and the Linux JanusGraph. Graph Technology is the backbone of Facebook and LinkedIn. It's also used to visualize complex data sets and to create visualizations like the ones below:

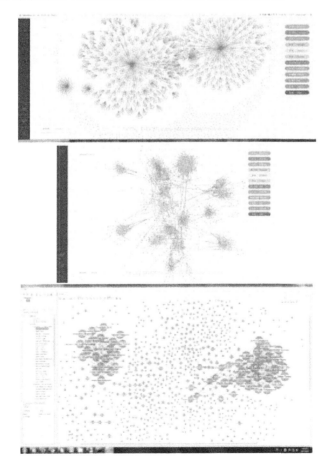

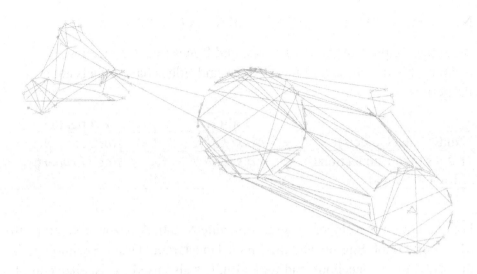

Above and below are visualizations of a real company using
https://ograph.io.

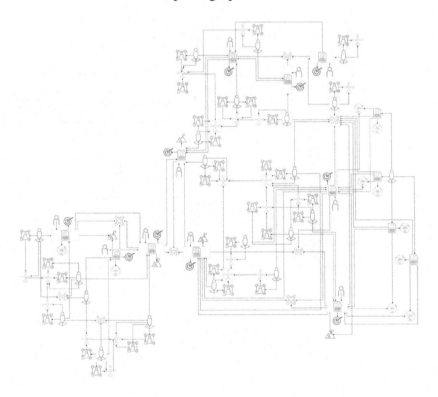

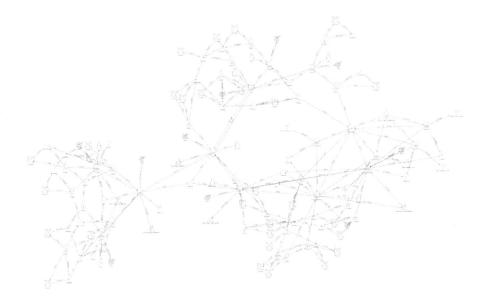

Above is the same company's Org Graph, just utilizing a different view / layout option. They can be color coded for clarity.

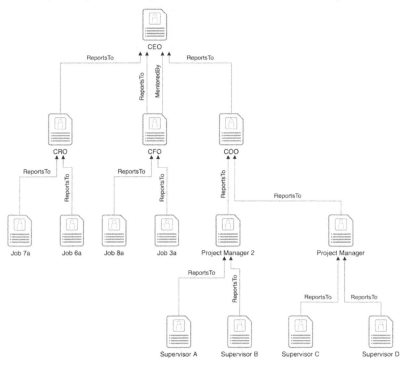

Above is the simple view of a classic org chart – yes, https://ograph.io has this view too.

7 QUESTIONS, 7 PROMISES, 1 ORGANIZATIONAL GRAPH

Before we move on from Jobs and Roles to a discussion of other key Nodes in the Organizational Cognizance Model, we want to return for just a moment to the Seven Questions and Seven Promises critical to cultivating engaged team members, detailed in my book, *The Patient Organization*. Over many years of coaching organizations, specifically polling and picking the brains of millennial ICs and doing all manner of soft-skills research, we arrived at the Seven Fundamental Questions that every team member wants to say *yes* to. Those questions are listed in the left-hand column below. The column on the right lists the corresponding answers organization must have to enable the Seven Promises that transform any organizations that has the guts to make and keep them.

The individual must say *yes* absolutely	The organization must say *yes* absolutely
1. **Do I belong?** (I fit the organization's core values and have the skill needed for my Job and Roles). **I Belong.**	1. We have clearly defined our core values and the skills necessary for every *Job* and *Role* are clearly laid out.
2. **Do I believe?** (I am motivated by the mission and the strategic direction leadership is taking). **I Believe.**	2. We know our *Why, our Focus,* and have a clearly mapped out strategy with priorities determined, laid out and shared.
3. **Am I Accountable?** (I understand and embrace the Purpose of my Job and Roles, what I should be thinking and doing). **Yes, I am Accountable.**	3. Our Accountability and Responsibility structure is clear. See the Organizational Cognizance Model 14 Point Checklist.
4. **Am I measured well?** (I understand and embrace how and why I am measured, I know what a good job is and agree with the metrics). **Yes, I understand and embrace how I am Measured.**	4. We have metrics, Objectives and Key Results for team members that inform them, giving them the latitude to form strategies to achieve these OKRs.
5. **Is my opinion is heard?** (I understand and embrace how my organization listens and how I my opinion is heard.) **Yes, I**	5. We have clearly mapped out and defined the communication channels we use to listen and communicate – our meetings,

understand and embrace how I am heard.	mentoring, etc. – build trust, spur debate and help our ICs grow.
6. **Am I being developed?** (I understand and embrace how my organization offers opportunities for development and I take an active role in my own development) **Yes, I understand and embrace how I am developed.**	6. We have clearly mapped out systematic development pathways for employees to participate in for their own development. This includes a combination of On-The-Job training, formal training, mentoring, coaching and accountability.
7. **Do I have balance?** (I understand and embrace what the organization's definition of balance is from a work-life, health and compensation perspective.) **Yes, I understand and embrace how my balance is maintained.**	7. We have taken the time to clearly define and communicate what work-life balance is to this organization and have communicated it up front with everyone. We have clear paths for employees to follow to maintain health and wellness balance and our compensation structures are clear and out in the open for the ICs to consider.

When ICs are answering *yes* wholeheartedly to these Seven Questions and organizations are diligently keeping these Seven Promises, you have Organizational Cognizance. We won't belabor the 7Qs and 7Ps here, since WE delve deeply into each of them, including the neuroscience, psychology and "heavy lifts" that help organizations get to *yes*, in *The Patient Organization*. Readers can get the 30,000-foot view of Organizational Cognizance in that book (and a more basic introduction at www.7q7p.com).

Death of the Org Chart is designed to be a practical companion to my earlier book, bringing the birds-eye view down to the ground and zooming in on the complicated pivotal question, number three. This question requires the IC to say, *Yes, I am Accountable. I understand and embrace for what I am Accountable.. I understand the Purpose of my Roles, what I should be thinking and doing* (remember the ultimate business question Peter Drucker supposedly uttered on his deathbed that we began the book with: *Who is doing what?* Now, it becomes, *what Role is doing what?*). It requires the organization to promise: *Our Accountability and Responsibility structure is clear.*

A quick sidebar about Accountability and Responsibility:

We should explain here that in our coaching and writing, We draw a distinction between "Accountability" and "Responsibility." You are *Accountable* for thinking – planning, considering, assessing a decision's potential impact. You are *Responsible* for doing – acting, executing, producing. Agreeing on these terms allows leaders and team members to clarify Accountabilities and Responsibilities. Do you understand and embrace both what you are Accountable for thinking about and Responsible for doing?

> **RACI** - This also ties to the usage of the words in the popular RACI model, where you map to **R**esponsible Parties, **A**ccountable Parties, Parties that need to be **C**onsulted and Parties that need to be **I**nformed. We are in essence capturing this approach in our OCM model, just in a much more detail that includes deeper context to understand why this Job or Role needs to be involved.

This book arose partly from my realization that ICs and organizations were often far from a *yes* on Accountability, that they couldn't see just how far from *yes* they were, and that the reason for this gap had everything to do with the inadequate and dated tool known as the Org Chart. Mention "Accountability" at most organizations, and people immediately reach for the old-fashioned Org Chart (and millennials cringe to see that it's bandied about on paper). We hope that our discussion of Roles demonstrated the Jobs-based Org Chart's massive shortcomings when it comes to clarifying Accountability in any way that's meaningful to ICs' daily work.

The Org Graph, with its flexible, dynamic view of Nodes and Edges, is much more functional. It grew from a combination of my desire to fill the gaping holes left by the old Org Chart (the desire to have ICs who are not just Accountable or aware, but Cognizant) and from my stumbling onto Graph Database technology. Without getting too technical, the same software technology we're using to visualize the Org Graph is used for lots of applications dealing with networks and relationships. Think of those amazing bubble charts you've seen showing groupings and connections – of devices, crime, income, voters, diseases. Medical officials use this technology to trace pandemics and Facebook uses it to follow networks of friends.

At its most basic level, the Graph has two elements, Nodes and Edges. Each Node represents an entity (in the Organizational Cognizance Graph Data Model, that means a Person, Job, Role, Meeting, Procedures/Work Inst./Polici, Workflow, etc.), and Edges indicate how Nodes are related (in the Organizational Cognizance Graph Data Model, that means: **ReportsTo, MentoredBy, Attends, InteractsWith, ResponsibleFor,** etc.). Details, attachments, videos, and file links coupled with Rich Text editors are built into each node for a colorful universe of information you can expand or contract with a click of a mouse.

Under the hood, things become much more complex, but this is about as technical as we need to get. The important point for our purposes is that, unlike other types of databases, with the Graph, relationships have primacy. They are every bit as important as the data records themselves. This is an important feature for achieving Organizational Cognizance, which depends on Individual Contributors understanding at a deep level exactly how they fit into the organization and relate to its many Systems, Processes, Mentors, Bosses, etc. on a daily basis.

GETTING YOUR HEAD AROUND KEY NODES AND EDGES

As we delve into the Organizational Cognizance Graph Data Model's specific Nodes and Edges, we will caution readers not to get too ambitious or ahead of themselves here. We've presented the Organizational Cognizance Model and Org Graph software enough to know that people immediately want to consider how it can be used from a management or leadership standpoint – an approach that can cause confusion. Though the Org Graph and Organizational Cognizance Model have a wide range of possible uses, keep it simple and begin by thinking, as we advised in Chapter 1, from the perspective of a new IC starting work. You share the Organizational Cognizance Model and her Org Graph with this new person, and she very quickly knows how to navigate the organization, what she is Accountable and Responsible for, who she communicates with for each Role, who will mentor her, what Processes she is a part of, etc. She won't achieve Organizational Cognizance right away, obviously, but she should hit the ground pretty damn aware by the end of that first week.

As we mentioned, we'll go through the mechanics of defining Roles, writing Role Purpose Statements, filling out a Role Capture Worksheet, etc. in Chapter 3, on facilitation. Once ICs have done that work, they map, with the help of colleagues and close supervisors, the key Nodes and Edges listed below to build out the Org Graph.

USING THIS SECTION OF THE BOOK AS A REFERENCE

I. Next to each Node is the icon that represents it in our Org Graph software, though, as we've said, the software is only one available tool, and the Organizational Cognizance Model doesn't depend on it. Readers can use whatever means they're most comfortable with to visualize their own Org Graphs.

II. Below each icon will be a paragraph, a written description describing the Node.

III. Below each of the Node written descriptions are graphics of its accompanying Edges. These graphics are screenshots from our software. They give a small taste – the best we can do on paper – of the ways that Nodes and Edges can be visualized in the Org Graph to build Organizational Cognizance and help ICs figure out where and how they fit. Edges are printed in bold in the paragraphs below and represented by arrows that indicate the type of relationship, or connection, between Nodes in the Graph. Those arrows can move in either direction, and follow specific rules depending on the nature of the connection.

PERSON: This is obviously the key component of any organization. The Organizational Cognizance Model always starts with and revolves around the person. The person **Owns** a Job. "Owns," as you can see from the graphic below is an "Edge," indicated by the arrow leading from the Person icon to the Job icon. We can personalize the Person Node with images and links to give it more life than just a name.

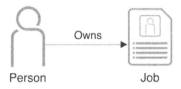

Job

JOB: We all know what jobs are, but in the Organizational Cognizance Model, we want to focus on the notion that a job is made up of various Roles. There are two Edges we must define for Cognizance. First, obviously, a Job **ReportsTo** another Job / Boss. This is a key Edge and, amazingly, the only piece of information from the Org Graph captured in the classic Org Chart. The second is **MentoredBy** – one's boss is not always his or her Mentor. We break the words Mentor and Coach apart. A Mentor is someone you turn to in confidence for guidance about your career or path in the organization. Ad-hoc Mentorship is not effective – spelling these relationships out is key. Consider a time when you worked somewhere, and your ad-hoc mentor left for another company. "Well, what am I, chopped liver?" you wondered, after all that time spent building a relationship that's now gone. Your second thought might have been, "I guess I better follow them…" Being overt about Mentoring is super healthy. A Job description, handbook, and other relevant material can be embedded, or uploaded in each Job Node and colored using Rich Text.

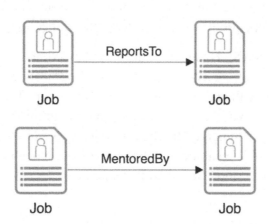

Role

ROLE: We have spent a good portion of this book so far explaining Roles and how they work in the Organizational Cognizance Model. Each Role is a function of a particular Job, so, in the Org Graph below, you can see that an Edge labelled **FunctionOf** points from the Role to the Job. In our basic Graph and starting view, the Role is the center of the universe (Org Graph views can be manipulated almost endlessly to clarify or emphasize relationships, a topic for later). Each Role is like an anchor and home for ICs, the vantage from which they see everything and the means through which they relate to all the Nodes that follow. The first Edge, or connection, for a Role is that it's a **FunctionOf** a Job, as noted above. The other Edges attaching Roles to various Nodes will be detailed according to the remaining Nodes below.

Role   FunctionOf   Job

Skill

SKILLS: Skills refers to the talents, abilities, and knowledge that qualify someone to do a Job or fill a Role. Degrees, certifications, licenses, etc. are not Skills but often indicate a set of necessary Skills. For instance, someone certified as a Microsoft Office Specialist should have the Skills to comfortably navigate Office programs. Other Skills, such as "effective communicator" are harder to quantify and are sometimes labelled as "soft." Two key Edges build Cognizance around Skills in an Org Graph. A Person **Has** Skills and a Job / Role **Requires** Skills. The gaps between these two Edges spell out for the IC and the organization exactly where someone might need work, Mentoring, training, or education. They highlight ICs who are overqualified for their Jobs and make good candidates for advancement, and they illuminate the path forward for ICs who want new challenges. If they're interested in Roles B and C or Job X, ICs can simply pull up the Org Graph, click on Skills for a Role or Job, and see exactly what they need to work on to get there. An employer can embed text, video, and links right inside a Skills Node, giving an IC direct access to training videos, online courses, manuals, etc. An IC can attach a CV or resume, links to certifications, degree programs, previous employers, etc, inside their Person node.

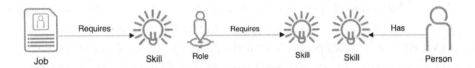

Bonus: Workforce Planning and Learning Management. Think about the Skills Nodes as a possible backbone for your LMS (Learning Management System) and as a Workforce planning tool. This utility was pointed out to me by Keith Langbo, of Kelaca. Keith's organization works with companies to define the skills / competencies required for different Roles and then matches the person with that level of mastery to the Role. Kelaca includes this in their KTAP (Kelaca Talent Advisory Program). For instance, Kelaca might rank someone as an MSExcel5, meaning he or she has demonstrated the top level of understanding and mastery of Excel. A Role may have a need for someone with MSExcel3 or higher, meaning a strong proficiency in Excel but not necessarily at the expert level, so this allows the team to identify people with the right skills for the right Roles & jobs, and can identify and lead towards resource development & training opportunities. Kelaca calls this part of their program, the KVPA or Kelaca Visual People Analyzer. This same tool & data can be utilized when looking at potential succession planning as part of the overall workforce planning efforts.

Imagine if each Skill Node contained the actual training material or a link to a system that administers the training, all right there in one place.

Role

COACH: Yes, we map this to another Role who is typically a SME (Subject Matter Expert). Who do I turn to with questions about my Role? In my experience, this Node is neglected even at the best-run organizations. Sometimes Coaching is an afterthought, and leaders simply assume it will happen (it won't, not adequately). Often, Coaching falls under an HR Job in charge of training or administration of the Learning Management System, but the person holding it doesn't know anything about 90 percent of the Roles ICs hold. Often, an IC has no clear idea who to turn to for help. The answer is Role Coach in the Organizational Cognizance Model, where Roles Coach other Roles. For instance, a new university accounting graduate gets a Job at a CPA firm, and her Job title is Staff Accountant. On a CPA Audit team, a Staff Accountant's Job might include the Role of Inventory Auditor. This Role is also held by an Advanced Staff Accountant – we would create Coaching Cognizance by linking these two Inventory Auditor Roles with the connection label (Edge): **CoachedBy**. The Org Graph spells out clearly who each Role is **CoachedBy**, guaranteeing clarity and speeding up the amount of time it takes to get to ROI.

Role   Role

Objective

OBJECTIVE: Objectives are the big-picture things we're aiming for, at the strategic level, and tend to be more qualitative than quantitative. (Note: when it comes to Objectives, the Organizational Cognizance Model ties into a strategy that Intel developed and Google extended called OKRs, or Objectives and Key Results. In essence, all strategic thinking is a cascade model, and you can use Organizational Cognizance and the Objectives and Results nodes to capture and visualize this type of thinking even of you don't follow OKRs exactly.). As we have explained, in the language of the Organizational Cognizance Model, we are "Accountable" for thinking when it comes to Objectives – planning, considering, building strategy, executing, making it happen, etc. – so the Edge for each "Objective" is labelled **AccountableFor**. Jobs can be **AccountableFor** Objectives and Roles can be **AccoutableFor** Objectives. Often in the OKR approach, there are "master Objectives" and "sub-Objectives," smaller Objectives that **Support** larger Objectives. If one Objective Node involves a new product, links to product info, marketing materials, sales targets, etc. can be embedded in the Node.

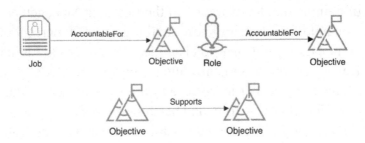

KEY RESULT: We are Accountable for thinking about Objectives, but *Responsible* for the actions that achieve Key Results. These Results are quantifiable – could include hitting a particular sales volume, retaining a higher percentage of clients, boosting website visitors by a certain number each month. The Edge connecting a Job or Role to a Key Result is labelled **ResponsibleFor**. In the OKR world, the basic measurement, the thing that has to be achieved, is the Key Result. Here, we are linking Key Results and Objectives with the edge, "**Enables.**" No, you do not have to be following OKRs to make Results and Objectives come alive. They are part of basic strategic thinking.

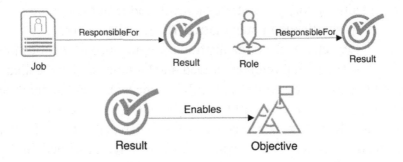

Team

TEAM: Data shows that the popular shift from hierarchical to more Team-centric models can improve performance, but according to a recent Deloitte survey, only 6 percent of respondents rated themselves very effective at managing cross-functional Teams. A major advantage of the Org Graph in today's environment is the ability to quickly display and manipulate "Team" Nodes. The Edge called **MemberOf** defines the relationship of a Role or Job to the Team that it's on.

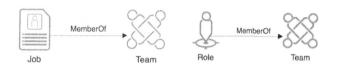

Meeting

MEETING: Meetings are an endless source of confusion and frustration for ICs. The Org Graph lays out visually exactly which Roles or Jobs **Attend** which Meetings. Note that it's the Role or Job, not the Person, that has the connection to, or Edge with, the Meeting. The IC can see at a glance that because he holds a Job called Sales Rep and is a Member of Team X, Participating in Workflow Y, etc., of course, he attends Meeting Z. All meetings should have a clear Purpose and Agenda, as we describe in *The Patient Organization,* but the starting point is getting every IC to understand how and why particular meetings matter for their Jobs and Roles, how they fit into the organizational fabric. The Org Graph is also a great tool for quickly spotting Roles or Jobs that should no longer be Attending certain Meetings – plus the useless Meetings that should be put to a quick death. A standing description of a Meeting can be embedded in a Meeting Node, and all relevant paraphernalia can be linked or attached – agendas, scorecards, to-do lists, etc. giving all ICs easy access.

Process

PROCESS: "Process" refers to all of the steps involved in passing tasks or information from one IC to another or one system to another for action according to procedural rules as value is added to the organization's activities. (You might call them Workflows too, but, BPMn 2.0 likes the term Process.) Processes have become more and more digitized and automated, so much so that they have become what we refer to as "invisible Processes", a trend that continues apace. This trend has added efficiency and saved organizations money, but it also can make these Processes invisible and make ICs feel removed from and confused by the Processes they're supposed to **ParticipateIn** because they cannot see the links in the chain any longer. The Org Graph once again ties the Workflow to the Role or Job, not the Person, to clarify how and why she **ParticipatesIn** it. We have two Edges for Workflow, the second is **Sub.** Sub means there is one Workflow that supports or flows into another Workflow. We can map and visualize these connection via our Graph.

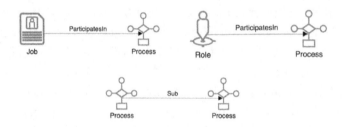

Procedure/WorkInst/Policy

PROCEDURES/WORK INST./POLICIES: A "Procedure/Work Inst./Policy" is usually attached to a Workflow as well as to a Role or Job. As you Participate in a Workflow, step one might be to **Follow** Procedures/Work Inst./Policy *A*, step two requires Procedures/Work Inst./Policy *B*, etc. The Org Graph allows you to see the overall Workflow, as well as the Procedures/Work Inst./Policies your Role **Follows** while Participating in that Workflow. The basic Org Graph below only shows a one to one Procedures/Work Inst./Policy connection – a Role or Job **Follows** a Procedures/Work Inst./Policy – but in reality it is a one to many situation, with a click of the mouse you can follow the edges and see who all is also attached to this Procedures/Work Inst./Policy, very important when it comes to changing a Procedures/Work Inst./Policy, we need to consider all parties involved with it, and upstream and downstream from it. Our software can display or hide other Edges leading from a Workflow to all its related Procedures/Work Inst./Policies. Here once again, links to videos, photos, diagrams, handbooks, etc. embedded in the Node for a complex Procedures/Work Inst./Policy can be invaluable for the IC.

Note: not show below is the **Maintains** edge, an important edge, we need to be able to see who has the domain and authority to update and maintain Procedures/Work Inst./Policies.

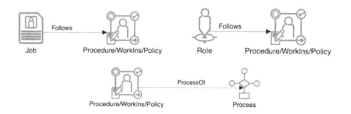

ENTITY: This is a broad group that captures a lot of thinking. Typically, an Entity is an element outside the organization proper or outside of the IC's functional unit, in internal customer for instance. A customer, vendor, contract or project could all be represented by an Entity Node. Likewise, if you're in Engineering but must deal with ICs in Field Surveying, this would be represented in your Org Graph as an Entity you **InteractWith**. We also use an Edge called **BelongsTo** in order to link Entities to Entities. One way to think of this **BelongsTo** edge is to capture the components of a large project with sub-projects. We can also use it as a map of the people in an external organization we **InteractWith**, a kind of level-to-level map that answers the question, *who is **InteractingWith** whom at client X? Imagine being able to share this detail with a confused client or IC?*

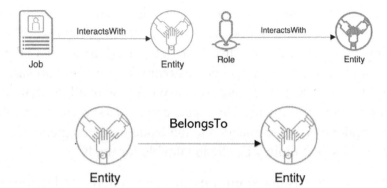

SYSTEM: In Organizational Cognizance Model language, we InteractWith Entities and **InterfaceWith** Systems. Again, since we're dealing with the limitations of print here and trying to keep things simple as we introduce concepts, the graphic below shows only one Node labelled "System." In 21st-century organizations, ICs often Interface with dozens of Systems, as we saw in the previous chapter, and a mouse click can display them all, with clear connections, or Edges, in our Org Graph. Generally, a system is any element – often digital these days, though not necessarily – in which an IC inputs data or work to have some function performed or info tracked. Salesforce.com, Quicken, the shared Excel spreadsheet a facilities manager uses to track building repairs, Google Hangouts – all qualify as Systems. Together, they often look like a fog-inducing bowl of alphabet soup to ICs, whose heads spin, trying to get a fix on HRIS, ERP, CRM, IMS, LMS…In an era of System proliferation, the Org Graph's ability to visualize how ICs interface with and relate to our many Systems is invaluable. Links to training materials, instructional videos, support sites, guides, etc. can be embedded in System Nodes.

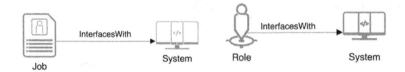

The descriptions above provide a basic overview to get readers started. They don't detail all of the views that an Organizational Graph can display, yet consider what an organization would look like if every IC had even the simplest version of this tool at her disposal from day one. Immediately, she would know all of the Roles that make up her Job, who **Coaches** her, what Teams she is a **MemberOf**, and what Processes she **ParticipatesIn**. She would be clear on the Objectives she's **AccountableFor**, the Results she's **ResponsibleFor**, all of the Meetings she **Attends**, and the Systems she **InterfacesWith**.

This IC would, on day one, understand in a meaningful way how she plugs into the organizational structure, how its key elements (Nodes) relate to her (through Edges), and to a high degree, how her work affects other team members and the overall organization. The Org Graph is a practical way to help all ICs understand three key elements explained in *Holacracy: The New Management System for a Rapidly Changing World* – Purpose, domain, and authority. As we'll see in the next chapter, we create a Purpose Statement for every Role, so ICs understand their *why* at a fine level. With the Organizational Cognizance Model and an Org Graph, ICs can also see what the appropriate domain, or sphere, is, not just for them personally, but for each Role they hold. They also know, within the context of their Roles, Accountabilities, and Responsibilities, exactly where their authority lies.

Developing this deep level of awareness into true Cognizance across the organization has a powerful, multiplying effect. Cognizance is cumulative. It accretes in beautiful ways. We call this the *Organizational* Cognizance Model, not the *Worker* Cognizance Model, because it's about achieving a deep level of transparency, clarity, and Purpose throughout the organization. Yes, ICs who are Cognizant of where and how they fit will be more engaged, but Teams will also work in greater harmony. Departments should better understand how their operations affect each other. Purpose cascades through various levels, linking the IC's Purpose with that of her team, unit, department, etc. – and with the overall organizational Purpose.

We dumped a lot of concepts and terms on you in this chapter, but we hope they grow clearer in the next, where we'll delve into facilitation and execution. This is the fun stuff for me and my firm. We spend most of our year walking organizations step by step through the exercises that allow them to build an Org Graph and implement the Organizational Cognizance Model and method.

NODE / OBJECT ICON SUMMARY

 Person   Job   Role   Objective   Result   Skill

 Team   Meeting   Entity   Process   Procedure/WI/Policy   System

CHAPTER 3

FACILITATION AND EXECUTION OF THE ORGANIZATIONAL COGNIZANCE MODEL

I apologize upfront – this section does not have a lot of color or entertainment, though it is the most useful, hands-on part of the book. In this chapter, we are going to roll up our sleeves and explore the concrete ways that the Organizational Cognizance Model helps organizations build Cognizance among ICs and answer the all-important question we started with – *who is doing what?*

As we've seen, answering this simple question clearly and thoroughly is incredibly difficult for a 21st-century organization – unless it's the size of Paul's Painting Company, payroll of one. Just as medical imaging harnessed technology to revolutionize diagnosis, though, the 3-D Org Graph uses Graph Database technology to visualize organizational complexity and build Accountability with a new level depth and clarity and this requires some hard work.

Organizational Orbits – You will hear the words "rings" when we describe organizations. We help our client think of their organizations using the analogy of a solar system or an atom, both have orbits around a center. We have rings that radiate out from the center that represent levels of the organization. You could say the sun at the center represents the Sr. leaders and the planets are Jobs and Roles orbiting the sun. Every now and then we might even have a comet that swoops in, cutting across orbits, that might be the board.

TAKING A FULL ROLE INVENTORY

[Note: We offer online self-lead video based learning courses on the following lessons and facilitations at https://organizationalcognizance.university]

Applying the Organizational Cognizance Method and building your own Org Graph takes some work upfront, though once you've done that work, the system can become largely self-maintaining and self-improving. We'll talk about maintenance in the next chapter, but first, we are going to give you a series of straightforward exercises that will allow you to create an

Organizational Role Inventory you will use to build Cognizance throughout the organization and to develop your own Org Graph.

These exercises don't require much more than a whiteboard, some time, and the will to face the complex reality of how your organization actually functions. We said above that the Organizational Cognizance exercises are straightforward, and they are, but this doesn't mean that they're easy. They involve looking at everything that needs to get done or thought about at your organization – every year, month, week, day, hour, second – you get the idea – then grouping these items into the right buckets, and making sure that nothing is slopping out or missing buckets altogether, dripping between them or through the cracks.

As part of the process, everyone, from the CFO to the newest IC, must understand and embrace *everything* that he or she is responsible and Accountable for (remember, in the Organizational Cognizance Model we're *Accountable* for thinking and *responsible* for doing). If you follow these Organizational Inventory exercises conscientiously and build your own Org Graph, you will be well on your way to Organizational Cognizance. You will have an organization where every IC understands the Roles she holds, as well as every Workflow, Procedures/Work Inst./Polici, and System she deals with. She will understand the function of every Meeting she **Attends** and exactly who she is **CoachedBy**. Her Teams, Objectives, Key Results, and all of the other complex Nodes and connections that the old Org Chart dumbs-down into a catchall box called "Job" will become crystal clear.

The Organizational Inventory of Roles we are about to walk you through demands that we focus primarily on Roles. Jobs aren't going away, but as we saw in the previous two chapters, Roles are the basic building block and starting point for the Organizational Cognizance Model. As an organizing principle, they are more precise and meaningful than "Jobs" and so, they give both ICs and leaders a clearer picture of *who is doing what* and how all the pieces connect.

As we'll see, thinking of each Role in terms of its own Objectives, Key Results, Meetings, etc. is enormously helpful in achieving Organizational Cognizance. Focusing on Roles, however, takes a mental adjustment if Jobs and People are your usual frame of reference. My advice is to remember that every Job is made up of Roles (recall our examples for Sales Director and Marketing Director in the previous chapter), and follow a simple rule when doing the first of these exercises: no proper names.

People fill Jobs. Roles are a **FunctionOf** a Job that is **Owned** by a Person. Roles are not named after people and neither are Jobs. Imagine even your dinosaur Org Chart only having the names of people. That would basically tell you nothing except who you report to, certainly not why. We want to assess each Role on its own merits, functions, necessity, etc. Part of the Organizational Cognizance process involves determining which Roles might be duplicating work or serving no real Purpose, which ones are attached to the wrong Job or require Skills that the current Role owners don't have. The whole point here is to step back and get outside the box, above the system for a fresh objective view. Describing a Role as "Tom's Role" gets us nowhere and undercuts that effort. It's also lazy and dodgy – watch for it.

Lazy Thinking – One serious habit we are encouraging you to try to break is the one where you use a person's proper name to describe the Role or Job that holds the responsibility or accountability. "That's Tom's Job" really means nothing and is lazy and really worthless language when you step back and look at this through the OCOG lens. Work hard to say something like this: "That is Tom's responsibility from his Role X."

THINKING OR DOING ROLES

In the graphic below we are trying to point out that in our experience Jobs have Roles that can be defined as *Thinking Roles* or *Doing Roles*, and can sometimes be a combination where their Purpose Statement will describe a combination of both. The language we use is *Accountable* for Thinking, (Strategizing, mapping.) and *Responsible* for Doing (Following the proven method, the process, not really challenged with improving, just do it.) We find that it is important to make this distinction. As you go more to the center of the organization, where leadership lives, these Jobs will have more Strategy and Thinking Roles linked to them where the front-line Jobs and their Roles, the ones out in orbit, will have more Responsible, Doing Roles as a general rule.

One of the weaknesses we find is this, as an organization grows, it creates new leaders from the Responsible Doers who have helped grow the firm, and, often these Doers do not understand that their Job now includes

Thinking Roles as well as their old Doing Roles. By sitting down with these leadership teams and running them through the Cracking Eggs and Pulling Teeth exercise, we are quickly and easily able to create a full inventory of the Thinking Roles the organization requires and assign these Thinking Roles to Jobs that are owned by the People around the table. This is a critical first step, because these Thinking Roles are Accountable for understanding the full OCM model as it relates to their Thinking Roles.

THE TWO FACILITATION METHODS:

For determining our mostly Thinking Roles, we can use *Cracking Eggs*.

For determining our mostly Doing Roles, we can use *Flower Power*.

CRACKING EGGS, PULLING TEETH, MAKING OMELETS

[Remember, there are online video lessons on the following items at https://organizationalcognizance.university]

Best method for determining Team Accountability (thinking) Roles

We call the first of our Organizational Cognizance facilitations "Cracking Eggs, Pulling Teeth, and Making Omelets." Yes, as the name implies, this one can get messy, even painful. To build our Org Graph and achieve Organizational Cognizance, we want to start with the inner ring in this exercise, the leaders around our Senior Leadership Team Table. This is the circle of people who hold mostly *thinking* Roles, those thinking about how and why we are doing what we are doing. From here, we'll expand to the outer rings of the organization, but we have to get Accountability, domain, and authority for these key thinking Roles straight first.

CRACKING EGGS

1. **Make a list.** Gather your senior leadership team (often, this is around eight people, give or take) to make a list on a whiteboard. Tell the Team to imagine that the table you're sitting around has a round dome top. Imagine thoughts, ideas, and issues as ball bearings. These ball bearings drop from the sky and hit our dome-topped table. What are they going to do? They are going to roll to the edge of the table. We ask this question: "To keep this company running and to get it to the future, what do we need to be thinking

about and doing every year, month, week, day, hour, second?" Any thought or issue that hits the dome-topped table is going to roll, and our goal here is to capture all of them with clear Roles, so nothing ever lands on the floor, slops over, or gets poured back and forth between Roles. List all of the things we need to be thinking about that can't slip between the cracks and hit the floor on your piece of paper. This list should cover everything you do, touch, consider, decide, communicate – everything that takes time. Leaders typically come up with 15 or so items each. So, if we have 8 people making a list, we will have 8 x 15=120 items to put on the board.

2. **Extract items.** Have a scribe extract the items on the team member's lists by standing at the whiteboard and going from one person to the next, asking, what is the one item you want to add to the list this time around? If someone says "sales and marketing," reply, "Nope, that's two, I asked for one." But still write these items down as the next two in the column before moving to the next person.

PULLING TEETH

3. **Group like items.** The next step can get a little painful, though like a trip to the oral surgeon, the payoff is well worth it. We are going to group like items in order to establish Roles. Once you have your list, start at the top left and put a #1 next to the first item. (Note: the numbers here are completely random – we're not prioritizing; putting a #1 next to an item does not mean it is the most important. We could just as easily use colors, shapes, or cartoon characters. The numbers are simply easy labels for grouping like items.) Ask the team to examine the items that make up your list, looking for things that seem to belong in the #1 grouping, or bucket. Have people identify similar items by calling out: "Column two, halfway down, item "x" is a #1. Place a #1 next to this item and the others the Team identifies as #1s.

   a. Common Question: "What if an item seems to fall into more than one bucket?" Normal question and simple, just put a dot (•) beside the # which keeps it "open" – •# (for instance, we could have one item labeled •#2•#4, which means we believe it belongs to both of these buckets and might belong to a third #. The • just means the item is open to accept other #s.)

4. **Keep numbering.** The next distinct item below #1 in the list will get a #2. Repeat the tagging exercise, with people calling out what else belongs in the #2 bucket and label those items with a #2. Move to the next unaddressed item down the list: it gets a #3. Find and label the other #3s, etc.

   a. Danger I: You will be tempted to skip forward and scatter your #3 and #4 and #5 across the board, Don't! Stay in the first column when assigning your first round of numbers, so that it will be easy to locate the first use of the number when it's time to name each grouping.

   b. Danger II: You will be tempted to name the numbers as you go along. Don't! Naming comes later. The point of the exercise is to stretch your brain, to keep it open and only think in buckets, using the numbering system to communicate. "That is a dot 3" is the correct language. Saying, "That is Marketing" is being lazy and short-circuits the process. You will get pushback from your lazy thinkers here; don't let the dim wits take over. Love, Walt

5. **Closing Dots Later:** The first goal in this step is to go through the entire list, examining only the items that aren't yet numbered. If something has a dot beside it, we will "close it out" with another number during the next pass. For now, just work to get a number or a number with a dot next to each item

Examples of a couple of boards with numbers in process, Dots that are still open.

Example of a board with all Dots "closed out."

The table below reflects the first four rows and three columns of the photo above as a finished numbered and dotted close out.

1 Getting Meetings	3•1•2 Market Knowledge	6•4•1 Emails
2 Mentoring	3•1•2 Market Education	6•4 Filing
1 New Busi Dev	1•4 Activity Tracking	4•6 Calendar Coordination
9•5•3•1 Client Follow up	5•9•1 Networking	3 R F Ps

MAKING OMLETTS

6. **Name the buckets.** The groupings, or buckets, that we've established are the framework for our Thinking Roles, which need to be named. Once every item is numbered, ask each person to take a sheet of paper and write the numbers down the middle, creating a left column area and a right column area. Label the left column "Humorous Role Name" and head the right column "Serious Role Name." Have everyone take a few minutes to think about and assign names to the numbers / buckets on his or her list. Often, the humorous column will follow a pattern, movies, cartoon characters. Why have a humorous column? The point is to stretch your brains, stretch your thinking, naming them twice, from two perspectives, drives deeper understanding and creates better outcomes; don't skip it.

    a. Next, pair people off by having them turn to the Team member to their left or right to discuss and compare lists. Each will typically agree to change a name or two as they compare their lists. Then have everyone turn to the person on his or her right or left side to discuss and compare lists. This gets people really focused and hurries things along. DO NOT skip this step.

    b. Split the group in two and have each half meet and come up with their favorite humorous and serious names.

    c. Set a whiteboard up with 4 columns and have a scribe from each group write his group's choices for these bucket names on the board.

d. Discuss the ideas with the whole group to find agreement on the best names. You might have to put some to a vote. Remember, this is still draft time. Nothing here is final, so don't sweat it. Also keep in mind that sometimes the humorous name is selected because it actually captures the essence of the Role.

e. Serious name tip: We have some clients who like to add "This is how we (fill in the blank)" to describe the essence of the thinking that will be filled by a leadership team member via their ownership of the thinking Role as a Function of their Job.

7. **Close out items.** Once you have this preliminary list of Role names, use it to "close out" the items with numbers and open dots, the things we couldn't definitively assign to one grouping the last time around. This means going back to the big list and armed with your bucket names and new understanding, adding a new number to an item that's still open (for instance, using the table above, let's say "•4 Activity Tracking" was hazy last time around but now agree the •4 will be closed out by adding a 1; we add the 1 and now we have "1•4 Activity Tracking" and we say it is "closed", no open •s.) or erasing the dot next to an existing number (we weren't sure if this was a 2, thus the dot, but we now agree that it is). Some items might belong to more than one group. If so, add another #. Assigning numbers to open items will be easy this time around because you will have a better handle on the groupings. You will find that some open dots are not covered with your current list, add a new #, name it on the fly and use it to close those dots. Normally 2 or 3 new numbers/Roles are added during this close out exercise.

8. **DANGER:** Resist the urge to cut the list down, grouping and eliminating numbers / buckets. This exercise is all about getting granular.

9. **Discuss Named Roles.** If you've been thorough in the steps above, the numbered "buckets" we just named on the board are the framework for your thinking Roles. In my experience, as we said, senior leadership teams typically have 10 to 14 vital thinking Roles after completing this exercise, sometimes as many as 25, depending on the complexity of what they do. As a group, talk about these Roles. Verbalize what you think the Purpose Statement for each

should sound like. Do the buckets, or Roles, seem airtight? Do they clearly define the owner's Purpose, domain and authority? Remember, you don't ever want a ball bearing, or an issue, to roll off the table, slip between Roles, and hit the floor. Nothing should get missed or neglected. It can't land and get passed back and forth between Roles either (when everyone's Accountable no one's Accountable). And it can't fall into a Role that's completely full and has no additional capacity – another recipe for neglect.

10. **Assign Thinking Roles to Jobs** (in essence, the leaders at the table). Now that the thinking Roles have been clearly established, assign them to Jobs in a way that senior leaders agree makes sense (remember, you're technically assigning to Jobs, not names or people at this point). For instance, you might determine that Roles named Social Media Strategies, Marketing Tactics, and Ad Budgeting all belong to the Job called Chief Marketing Officer. The Person who currently fills that Job owns all of those thinking Roles, and everyone now knows it. Another Role called Risk Management belongs to the CFO Job. Other people can and should still think about risk, but the CFO owns this Role. It is his domain, and he has the authority on risk. The buck will stop with him on this issue, and everyone knows it.

		How We			
Skippy	1	Do the Crew for the Day		Skippy	Ray
Kim	2	Maintain Inventory		Kitchen/Front	
Skippy	3	Do the Daily Grind	Food	Mowing	Merch	Parking
Ray	4	Do Family Service		Patty	Roy	Ray
Ray	5	Do Daily Checklist		Front	Outside
Mindy	6	Embrace Unique			
Kim	7	Accounting Record Keeping			
Mindy	8	Food Consistency + Quality			
Matt	9	How we make money on everything we sell			
Skippy	10	Make Waldo Happy			
Ray	11	Makin the Cut			
Kim	12	Crap Master-Admin			
Mindy	13	Under the Big Top			
Mindy	14	Friendly Outreach			
Matt	15	Facilities			
Matt	16	Nursery			
Matt	17	Crew- Acq-Train-Retain-			
Kim	18	IT-Software			

Example of #s Named, with a person linked to each. This is a real company's list.

Leaders will leave this facilitation with a much better sense of everyone's domain, authority, and Purpose when they are meeting around their leadership table. People will be Cognizant of the many things that absolutely have to be thought about strategically and dealt with monthly, weekly, daily, hourly – and exactly who is Accountable for thinking about each. Bobby owns the Job of CFO, so he is the keeper of our strategies regarding risk. Bobby knows this, and if anyone has a question or concern involving risk, they know that Bobby in his CFO Job is the Person to talk to.

When Bobby worries about something that raises our risk profile, everyone is also Cognizant of the fact that he's approaching the issue from his Role of Risk Management, and they appreciate the thinking this involves. Bobby, in turn, knows that Lisa, the Chief Marketing Officer, is approaching the same issue through her Role of Marketing Tactics and the risk thinking that underlies it. Their interaction is more informed – and often less tense – because, excuse the cliché, each is Cognizant of the other's Role, and thus where the other is coming from.

As we wrote in the previous chapter, the sailor in me can't help thinking of this dynamic in terms of what, in navigation, we call "triangulation." You see something from a particular Role, your bearing; somebody else looks at it from their Role, or bearing, and together, you can get a precise fix on that thing. The Team is more focused, and if Roles are being taken seriously, tasks stop slipping through the cracks.

ROLE PURPOSE STATEMENTS (for both Thinking and Doing Roles)

Once you have your Roles *Named*, The Role Purpose Statement is a very important step. To get to Organizational Cognizance, people must understand the Purpose of each of their Roles. we advise leaders to follow Simon Sinek's simple yet powerful formula to craft these Purpose statements: *Why? How? What?*

If you're familiar with Sinek's work, you know that he argues that the *Why,* or Purpose, should be the first priority for any business or organization – and we would add, for any Role. Take his advice and "start with *Why.*" Why does this Role exist? What is its Purpose? Why is it important to my Job and to the overall mission of the organization?

Leaders are generally familiar with the *What* – closely connected to the Objectives listed in the Worksheet below. What should this Role achieve – whether that's a particular standard, a kind of service, or a product? Finally, think about *How* we get there? How do you go about fulfilling a particular

Role's Purpose and reaching the *What*? This question is closely tied to the Results column in our Worksheet.

These Purpose statements are important, but they must also be simple and succinct. One to three sentences should do it. Here are a couple examples drawn from our hypothetical leaders above:

> *The Purpose of the Social Media Strategies Role is to boost our online presence and leverage word of mouth to augment our marketing efforts with minimal expenditure. This is mostly a Thinking Role where I am tasked with thinking and strategy around how the organization does Social Media.*

> *The Purpose of the Risk Management Role is to be accountable for identifying and evaluating risks organization-wide and then responsible for executing strategies and applying resources to minimize them while maximizing opportunities.*

> *The Purpose of this Role X is primarily accountable for thinking about and forming strategies and processes that the organization can form around and follow to execute.*

> *The Purpose of Role Y is primarily responsible for executing the plans and following the processes that are determined in Role X.*

Why, What, How, use your common sense, your common judgement here. My grandfather, who owned a classic general store in a one-stop-light town in the early 1900s used to tell a story of three older gentlemen sitting on the front porch of the store in rocking chairs, playing chess and watching the world go by. Along came Billy Williams, fresh from university, driving by in his new Chevy convertible…One rocking chair gentleman said to the group: "Well, thar goes Billy Williams, he's got a ton of book larnin' but not a lick of common judgement." Don't overthink this stuff.

THE FLOWER POWER EXERCISE

[Remember, there are online video lessons on the following at https://organizationalcognizance.university]

Best method for determining IC Responsibility (doing) Roles

We started with the inner ring, the thinking Roles that steer the ship, by having leaders do the Eggs, Teeth, Omelets exercise and fill out Organizational Cognizance Role Capture Worksheets for each of their thinking Roles. Once those Roles have been established, we do a similar exercise for all ICs, leaders to line workers, to get a grip on their Roles and build Cognizance throughout the organization. Here's how the Flower Power exercise works:

1. Gather a group of ICs with the same or very similar jobs who work together. If, for instance, the organization has four Client Service Agents, they would make a group. Include a supervisor or manager in this meeting to facilitate, but make sure it's someone close to the work, with direct knowledge of what's going on. Caution: bringing in someone who's two levels removed can do more harm than good here.

2. Decide randomly who you will start with and write that person's name in the center of a circle on a whiteboard. Let's say that Cheryl is going first.

3. The Cracks Question: Now ask the team to reflect on what Cheryl does, everything that she's thinking about and doing – every month, week, day, hour, second. What are all the things on Cheryl's plate that have to get done or thought about, that can't fall through the cracks? Have people make a list and have Cheryl do the same.

4. Extract and Group on the Board: Next, go around the group and have each person share one thing that Cheryl does. The first person might say, "answering client calls." Write that on the board. The next person might say, "sending welcome packets to new clients." Write that in another area on the board. If the next person says, "answering client emails," you might decide as a group that this belongs in the same area as "answer client calls." Jot it down there.

5. Keep going around: Keep going around the group, jotting down list items and grouping similar ones in the same area on the board. By the time you've gone through everything that Cheryl does – all that

she thinks about and every task she completes every second of every day – and grouped them in similar areas, you might have half a dozen or so of these buckets / groupings.

6. Petals: Finally, loop each group back to Cheryl with an oblong line that surrounds it anchoring both ends on the central circle. The resultant diagram will look like a flower with long petals – thus the name of the exercise. The petals are Cheryl's Roles, each of which is looped back to the center, to Cheryl, where they overlap with each other to form her Job.

7. Number the petals and go through the naming exercises and Organizational Cognizance Role Capture Worksheet as explained in steps 10 and 11 of the Eggs / Teeth / Omelets exercise above.

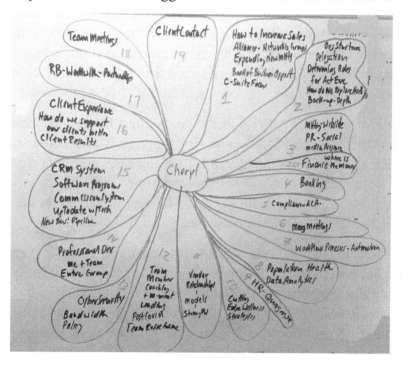

An example board of a Flower exercise showing all the things that take up Cheryl's day. There are more examples of boards in the appendix.

Like the Cracking Eggs exercise that began this chapter, the Flower Power Exercise allows you to establish the Roles that make up Jobs, in this case for the outer rings of your organization, the Roles that impact ICs the most. After clearly defining Roles in this way, everyone leaves the room with a deeper understanding of his or her own domain, authority, and Purpose – along with everyone else's.

As with the leadership Team in our earlier example, in this one, the Client Service Agents are now deeply aware of the priorities that must be acted on or thought about every month, week, day, hour, and second. And they now have clarity on exactly who is Accountable for doing or thinking about each of those things (note that in the Organizational Cognizance Model, we're continually answering Peter Drucker's key question: *Who is doing what?*).

Questions of time capacity will inevitably arise during this exercise, too. Building and then reviewing these Flower Diagrams, for instance, our hypothetical organization's Client Service Agents might determine that Cheryl's Roles are too full and things are slipping through the cracks, while Ron has room to do more. If people are overwhelmed, not pulling their weight, out of their lane, etc., it's much more likely to come to light in discussing Roles as we build our Org Graph than in reviewing Jobs on an Org Chart.

After the Flower Power exercise, ICs should write a Purpose Statement and fill out an Organizational Cognizance Role Capture Worksheet for each of their Roles, just as leaders did after the Cracking Eggs exercise (see above). we won't reprint the Worksheet here or repeat how to fill it out, since the sheet and process are exactly the same for delivery drivers as for the CFO and should be leveraging common sense.

Yes, *everyone* at the organization has to fill one of these out for every Role he or she holds in the Organizational Cognizance Method. Is it really important for a receptionist or groundskeeper to be Cognizant of their Purpose and Roles? Do they really need Coaches? Yes, yes, and yes. As we've said many times now, an organization is a fiction, only given meaning and power by those who believe in it. To be a Cognizant Organization, that belief must extend from the corner office to the factory floor.

Why? For starters, today's mailroom worker might very well be tomorrow's comptroller or vice president of sales. This is real. One of my client's, Julia, started as a receptionist at Allina Health in Minneapolis, MN and now holds a VP Role. She started fresh out of school in 2007 and worked her way up – amazing! All workers want to say, yes, they feel that they are being developed – the sixth of the Seven Questions critical to cultivating culture and engaged team members. Building Cognizance among frontline workers helps you to build a bench, maximize resources, and groom leaders in-house. It also boosts motivation and engagement throughout the organization.

More important, though, the foundation of the Organizational Cognizance Model and the Org Graph is transparency and clarity for *all* ICs, the entire organization. When you begin thinking that Cognizance is only for leaders or for ICs above a particular paygrade, you might as well return to the old Org Chart. In that case, you are essentially taking the Blue Pill, to recall our *Matrix* example, dozing off, and allowing people to believe whatever they want.

Any place that you decide doesn't need Cognizance – the reception desk, loading dock, mailroom – becomes a blind spot, a potential haven for dysfunction and a drag on the organization. It only takes one blind spot to cause a traffic fatality, one short circuit to screw up an entire electrical system. The whole premise of the Org Graph is that organizations thrive with a full 360-degree 3-D view. The Org Graph is an incredible tool, but it is only as good as the data it's built on. Building a good Org Graph means *everyone* working hard on the exercises above in a spirit of openness and inclusion.

THE ORGANIZATIONAL COGNIZANCE ROLE TO 14 POINT MATRIX - WORKSHEET

In the Organizational Cognizance Model, the Worksheet below is used both with senior leaders, who hold largely thinking Roles; and with the farthest rings of frontline workers, who hold mostly "doing" Roles; and everyone in between.

After the Flower Power and Cracking Eggs, Pulling Teeth, and Making Omelets exercises above, teams fill out an Organizational Cognizance Role to 14 Point Matrix to capture and locate each Role that is a **FunctionOf** of the Job they **Own**. You'll note that the line items on the Matrix track the "Nodes" we introduced in the previous chapter. A simple Excel spreadsheet works well for collecting this data, which will provide the foundation for your Org Graph.

We should note that some Roles might not need to connect to every Node in the model. There could be a Role, for example, that is not a **MemberOf** any Team or that doesn't **Attend** any regular Meetings. In such cases, the space for Nodes that don't apply can simply be left blank.

Defining and naming Roles through the exercises above is a good start, but don't make the mistake of assuming that this means people are truly Cognizant of them. The Organizational Cognizance Role To 14 Point Matrix Worksheet helps everyone, leaders and ICs alike, to dig deeper, interrogating each Role he or she owns, thinking about why it exists, what it should accomplish, and every Node it connects with – all relevant Meetings, Systems, Procedures/Work Inst./Policies, Processes, etc.

We have argued throughout this book, that an organization is a fiction, given power by those who believe in it. This does not mean, however, that we should expect blind faith. The belief we are describing is a result of knowledge, awareness, and connection. If people don't understand on a deep level what they're being asked to believe, faith is impossible. The Org Graph that we'll build from the Organizational Cognizance Role Capture Worksheet acts as a kind of organizational bible, shining a light on how things work and providing a map for how to operate. Like a bible for the faithful, the Org Graph is also a living tool, a place to turn for answers, a daily source of revelation.

Belief demands Cognizance, as we said in Chapter 1, and unpacking each Role is a key step to building both.

ROLES TO 14 POINT MATRIX WORKSHEET - Blank

	Primary Job	Role 1	Role 2	Role 3
Job				
Report To				
Coached By				
Teams				
Meetings				
Entities				
Processes				
Procedures/Work Inst./Policies				
Systems				
Objectives				
Key Results				
Skills				
% A or R**				

ROLES TO 14 POINT MATRIX WORKSHEET - Completed

	Primary Job	Role 1	Role 2	Role 3
Job	Job A	Job A	Job C	Job A
Report To	Job B (Tom)	Job B (Tom)	Job D (Anne)	Job B (Tom)
Coached By	-	P4 SME*	P5 SME	P6 SME
Teams	Team A	"as job"	Team B	"as job"
Meetings	Meeting A	"as job"	Meeting B	"as job"
Entities	-	E1	-	E1
Processes	-	WF1	WF2	WF1
Procedures/Work Inst./Policies	-	P1	P3	P2
Systems	-	S1, S3	S2	S1, S3
Objectives	Obj A	"as job"	O2	"as job"
Key Results	-	KR1, KR2	KR5, KR6	KR3, KR4
Skills	-	Skill 1, Skill 2	Skill 5	Skill 3, Skill 4
% A or R**	See Roles	80/20	25/75	10/90

Note: SME* - Coaches are often Subject Matter Experts, they have a Role: Subject Matter Expert – Coach.

BONUS LINE: % A or R** What we are asking on this line is to estimate the amount of time a Role spends in Thinking (Accountable) or Doing (Responsible) the total is always 100%

How Instructions: We are assuming that you have made some Omelets and completed your Flower Powers and have written your Role Purpose Statements, so, we a are no longer debating the Roles at this point.

This can be a little hard to get started, but, once the teams get moving it flows.

We start with building a matrix as above on a whiteboard on inside a spreadsheet. (note: for this exercise we leave out "mentored by")

1   First Step: We set a base line by going down the Primary Job stack first. Often Coached by is left blank because coaching is more Role based, or Teams is left blank because Roles are part of teams, not Jobs. Each organization is different.
2   Second Step: We fill in the matrix for each Role.
    a. This information is what we will use to complete the Org Graph.
    b. One thing we are looking for is where a Role really does not fit under the "Primary Job" – when it is more of an outlier. We will sometimes see we need to add a new Job, or put the Role elsewhere.
    c. Another thing we are looking for are the patterns of how we will use the Org Cog model. We are asking questions like: "Our meetings, are they more Job centric or Role centric."
        i. Remember the goal is reality, granularity.

Refer back to our list of Nodes in Chapter 2 for help filling in each of the columns in the Role to 14 Point Matrix above. Most are fairly obvious, though organizations might use some terms differently than we do in the Organizational Cognizance Model. "Objectives," for example, refer to big-picture qualitative stuff in the argot of Organizational Cognizance – strategic thinking, planning, execution of long-term goals. "Results" are more controllable – a sales call volume, a client retention visits, the number of new accounts per quarter. Some readers might use these words interchangeably in daily life, so the distinction is important.

We are **AccountableFor** Objectives (emphasis on thinking) and **ResponsibleFor** Results (emphasis on doing).

Processes, Procedures/Work Inst./Policies, and Systems are also closely related and might cause confusion for some readers, depending on how those terms are used at their organizations. In the world of Organizational Cognizance, you can think of a Workflow as a river. What route does work take as tasks or information flow from one IC, department, unit, etc. to another for some action as your organization adds value to a product or service? Procedures/Work Inst./Policies are like docks along that river route, where a boat might stop for fuel, food, a paintjob, a cargo inventory, new maps…These are the protocols that get followed to move a task through the workflow. As noted earlier, Step 1 in a Workflow is often to follow Procedures/Work Inst./Policy *A*, Step 2 involves Procedures/Work Inst./Policy *B*, etc. We **ParticipateIn** Processes and **Follow** Procedures/Work Inst./Policies.

Our many Systems involve inputting data or work of some sort to have a function performed or info tracked (think Salesforce.com, Quicken, Google Hangouts, etc.). The **Workflow** of servicing a new client would involve a variety of **Procedures/Work Inst./Policies**, the first of which might be entering them into your CRM **System**. The connections between Nodes, as you can see, is complex and often difficult to picture clearly (impossible on an Org Chart). The Organizational Cognizance Role to 14 Point Checklist Matrix Worksheet helps us think about the moving parts inside each Role individually, how they relate to each other, to the Job, the Person, and the organization.

Words, however, can only do so much. The real magic occurs when this data is transferred into a 3-D Org Graph that allows people to visualize all of this complexity – the soup they swim in daily – in a way that's clear and comprehensible at a glance.

Once you finish your Role Inventory, Role Purpose Statements and the Roles to 14 Point Matrix you are ready to upload your data into OGraph.io

THE 14 POINT CHECKLIST SUMARY PAGE (is the result)

Person	

Job	Reports To	Mentored By

Roles		Coached By

Teams	Meetings	Entities

Objectives	Key Results	Skills

Processes	Procedures/Work Inst./Policies	Systems

BUILDING AN ORG GRAPH

After you complete the Organizational Cognizance Role Inventory exercises and Role to 14 Point Matrix, you can begin building your Org Graph. We have said from the start of the book that you do not have to use our Organizational Graph software to build your Graph, and that's true. You do, however, have to find a way to visualize the complex organizational data you now possess. Lists and spreadsheets won't get you to Cognizance. Neither will static diagrams.

You need a way to see all the relevant Nodes (Processes, Systems, Procedures/Work Inst./Policies, Coaches, Meetings, Teams, etc.) and their unique relationships, or Edges (**ParticipatesIn, AccountableFor, Owns, InteractsWith, Attends,** etc.) clearly, at a glance. Yet another list or spreadsheet will add *complexity* not *clarity* to the plates of overburdened ICs. It will become another "Slogin," as my client says, on the already enormous list of apps, Systems, communications channels, etc. that ICs navigate on a daily basis. This is the opposite of what we want to do in the Organizational Cognizance Model.

Furthermore, ICs and leaders must be able to interact with and manipulate the data under this visualization. To move you toward Cognizance, the visualization must reflect the reality of how your organization and its ICs function – that's the whole point. If your organization is anything like the hundreds we've worked with over the years, then it functions in ways that are complex – dare we say *messy* – and constantly evolving. Team members must be able to see this reality in real time, not some idealized or dumbed-down version of their Job that's perpetually out of date. They must see the big, organization-wide picture and be able to zoom in on the parts of the visualization relevant to questions they have about a particular Team they're a **MemberOf**, a Meeting they **Attend** for Role A, a Coach who offers advice on Role B, a System they **InteractWith** out of Role C…

A static diagram can't capture the complexity of a single Role, much less the hundreds of interrelated Roles and thousands of relationships that make up even a small organization. If you're attempting to capture what we've been talking about in a static two-dimensional diagram such as an Org Chart, you are more than likely frustrated. An Org Graph must be three-dimensional, yet easy to use and comprehend. A new hire should be able to interact with it on her first day, maybe even before her first day, since, you'll recall, fast onboarding is one of its chief benefits.

The list of criteria we've just named has enormous benefit for the user – an IC trying to understand her Roles, how her organization actually functions, how she fits – but it's a tall order for the software developer. In refining the Organizational Cognizance Model over the years, even I knew that, and I am by no means a software expert, or even much of a computer guy. From working my first job in accounting to running multiple businesses to coaching organizations today, I have learned whatever computer magic I needed as I needed it. If I had a problem, I looked for a digital tool that could solve it. I don't browse for apps or systems or new communication channels unless it's to address a specific issue. Life in a modern organization is complicated enough (see Chapter 1). Who has time for an app solution in search of a problem?

In the case of the Organizational Cognizance Model, we had a significant problem – how to visualize all of the complex organizational elements and relationships we've been discussing, the stuff we have spent years coaching leaders about, in a way that met all of the criteria above. We have been using the exercises and Organizational Cognizance Role to 14 Point Matrix Worksheets presented in this chapter for some time, and they are always helpful, but we knew that without a way to visualize, interact with, and constantly update organizational dynamics in three dimensions, our other tools would continue to fall short on delivering true Organizational Cognizance.

ON A NAPKIN, LIKE EVERY GREAT SOLUTION

I mentioned this challenge to a family friend, Elias Hicks, a twenty-seven-year-old Princeton grad and data wonk who had moved back to North Carolina's Research Triangle and was looking for a job. We met at a Starbucks to talk over his career options and which contacts I might introduce him to. Once that conversation wound down, I sketched the Organizational Cognizance Model on a napkin, explained what I wanted to achieve, and he immediately said, "Oh, that's a Graph Database. It's a perfect fit. I can model that up for you in Neo4j."

We hired him to build a basic model. Once we saw how Graph Database technology worked and shared it with a few clients, we understood that this software solution was exactly what we were looking for.

THE MAGIC OF COLLABORATION

We put the project out to bid, and, unfortunately, building even a basic Graphic User Interface with the functionality we needed was exorbitantly expensive. My dream seemed to be dying on the vine. Like a dog fixed on a bone, though, we were not willing to give up that easily.

One day, I found myself browsing around deep inside some AWS information, and I stumbled across a Berkley-based software company called Tom Sawyer Software that had roots in IBM Watson and three decades of data and layout experience, with a client list that included the likes of Toyota, 3M, and Boeing. They happened to be rolling out a dazzling new Graph Database product called Perspectives, which was an ideal solution for the Organizational Cognizance Model. My challenges, in turn, were of exactly the type that Tom Sawyer wanted to solve with Perspectives. I "LinkedIn" to their CEO, Brendan Madden, gave him a call, quickly explaining what I had in mind, and Brendan said, "Let do it." Madden and I formed a collaboration, a joint venture, and the Org Graph was born on my years of organizational structure experience and Brendan's team of world-class developers. It now lives at https://ograph.io.

CLICK, DRAG, BUILD

Tom Sawyer Software's Perspectives product is very much under the hood and behind the scenes when it comes to ograph.io, our Organizational Graph solution, and the Organizational Cognizance Model. We bring this up to give credit to a talented partner who helped build and now supports exactly what we need to replace the old Org Chart and achieve Organizational Cognizance.

I'm also sharing this journey in order to highlight all that's needed for an effective Org Graph and to acknowledge that this is a team effort. There might be another way to build an Org Graph and effectively visualize the Organizational Cognizance Model short of spending millions of dollars to develop your own basic user interface for an existing Graph Database program. However, we are not aware of anything as of this writing that has a Graph Data Model built from real-world, real-team, real-IC experience coupled to a world-leading platform.

ADP, the big payroll giant, is rolling out a "Skunk Works" project that includes a graph approach to team visualization, showing Persons on Teams. This is super exciting for us. Why? Because in my experience, if you have a great "unique" idea or solution, someone somewhere out there in the world likely has the same idea. Unless that someone is a troll in a hole, you have an opportunity to ride that solution wave together. ADP is certainly not a troll.

The Org Graph Data Model and software solution we have developed meets the criteria we have outlined with flying colors. It allows ICs to visualize all of the complexity of their Roles and Nodes and the web of connections linking them in ways that are clear, interactive, and easy to digest. Our software makes it simple to build your own Org Graph (you can have a basic structure done, literally, in minutes) and to update it in real time.

Someone once said that writing about music is like dancing about architecture (if you are having trouble with this metaphor, picture the hated mime, acting out on a street corner what a building will look like). Writing about software is equally awkward and inadequate. The best way for you to see how our Organizational Cognizance software works is to take five minutes and go to https://orgaph.io. There, you can watch a couple of short demos that walk you through the simple process of getting started on an Org Graph of your own. You can also take the system for a test drive and play with the features.

As you'll see at our website, the Organizational Graph software presents you with a big blank pallet, or canvas, to start. We have a menu across the top, one down the middle, and an outline of your work with filter options down the left side. The interface functions a lot like Photoshop. The top row allows you to interact with and visualize what you create on the canvas in various ways. The menu down the center is your drop-and-drag objects menu, the bottom icon is the Edges tool you use to connect Nodes. On the left are interactive outlines that represent the Nodes and Edges we have arrived at through our exercises and Organizational Cognizance Role Capture Worksheets – Person, Job, Role, Objective, Key Result, Team, Meeting, Workflow, etc.

To get started building an Org Graph, a user simply clicks on a Node icon from the middle object menu, drops it on the drawing pallet, and then connects it using the simple, intuitive Edge tool – at the bottom of that same menu. This tool allows you to draw a line between Nodes and show the nature of the relationship. Click on the Node for Person and then click onscreen, and the Person icon pops up (we introduced these icons in Chapter 2). Click on the Job Node and then on screen, and a Job icon pops up. Use the Edge tool to connect them and a line automatically appears, labelled **Owns:** this Person **Owns** this Job.

INSIDE EACH NODE LIVES RICH, SEARCHABLE DETAIL

Rich, searchable details and text lie underneath each and every Node. It's super important to create a universe of color and depth in each Graph Node. Right click on your Node to rename it, write a short description, color-code it, upload a video or file, link it to a file or outside URL. Choose the Rich-Text tab and you can add searchable Rich-Text pages that support not only the text of your choice but also embedded videos, links, picture, files, etc.

From here, users simply click to add and drag to connect the Objectives, Key Results, Teams, Meetings, Processes, etc. attached to that Job. Next to one Job, you can click to create another Job that the first Job **ReportsTo**, and then another that this Job is **MentoredBy**, since the reality is that we're not always mentored by the person we report to.

From each Job, you can then click to create the Roles connected to it, labelled with the Edge **FunctionOf**. Around each Role, click on Nodes and Edges to quickly create all of the Meetings, Processes, Teams, Procedures/Work Inst./Policies, Systems, Entities, Objectives, etc. attached to it. All of this data has been established through our Cracking Eggs and Flower Power exercises and the Organizational Cognizance Role Capture Worksheets in this chapter. With a couple of clicks, you can create visualizations for the attendee list associated with a Meeting Node, a diagram associated with a Workflow, a video link related to a Procedures/Work Inst./Polici, a checklist linked to a Role…

Simple, right? Well, it's even simpler once you're in the Organizational Cognizance software and clicking away, which is why we are encouraging you to go to https://ograph.io for a better demonstration than we can provide in these pages. Within a few minutes, you can create a visualization that captures the complex web of an IC's Job and Roles, her many functions and connections within the organization.

We are not even going to touch on many of the features built into the Organizational Cognizance software, including the multitude of views and layouts – symmetrical, circular, classic, hierarchical, orthogonal, etc. – that allow you to see Jobs, Roles, and the organizational structure from various useful perspectives. Switching views takes only a mouse click, but the new point of view that results from the shifting of Nodes and Edges – a kind of 3-D organizational ballet on your screen – is one of the more impressive features of our Graph Database software. It must be seen to be appreciated, and we don't want to muck it up by attempting to capture it in words.

With filters, we can declutter or drill down into the particular view and information we want. Just go to the left-hand objects outline area and click on the word "filters." From here you can check boxes with a click to hide or show whatever Nodes and Edges you want.

A leadership team or hiring manager can color code the Org Graph to envision different scenarios, creating almost endless opportunities to learn more. By the time this book is out, we also will be embedding analysis tools that you can use to, well, analyze your organization.

It all starts with doing the Organizational Inventory work in this chapter.

Having an IC start a new Job with access to this clear visualization of exactly where she fits and how things function – every Meeting, System, Procedures/Work Inst./Policy, and Workflow she touches – accelerates onboarding and ROI, boosts performance and Accountability. Once every Job and Role is accurately represented in a 3-D Org Graph, the benefits multiply exponentially as you achieve Organizational Cognizance. In the next and final chapter, we'll explore the benefits of an Org Graph and the Organizational Cognizance Model, and how to maintain them.

CHAPTER 4

ORGANIZATIONAL COGNIZANCE

RESULTS YOU CAN LEVERAGE AND MAINTAIN

We will start this chapter with a couple of complexity stories to illustrate how the Org Graph builds Organizational Cognizance and helps you achieve concrete results.

Example 1: Who is doing what, with whom, when, and how does it all flow?

The first story involves a client of ours in the financial planning business. Somewhere around 80 percent of U.S. workers do all of their financial planning at work, and this client, who we will call Smith Planning, helps organizations and their employees with everything from standard employee benefits to life insurance to retirement planning to financial planning. Smith Planning has the following belief statement: Everyone deserves the opportunity to be led to financial freedom.

Smith is typically hired by a company, its "client," but once that happens, it also has a raft of sub-entities beneath that client – the client's employees, who Smith Planning works with individually. The company as a client has certain needs and requirements and each employee also has his or her own unique financial situation and a set of particular needs and goals. Smith offers the client and its employees four distinct service lines, and it has SMEs (Subject Matter Experts) in each who serve that area within Smith but also serve both the client and the client's employees.

Are you counting Nodes and doing the Nodes squared minus the number of Nodes complexity math?

Think about the number of Nodes and relationships this business model creates, the complex Processes, Systems, and Procedures/Work Inst./Policies involved. The number of Roles grows quickly, and even the ones that might seem disparate are tightly connected, since financial planning has to work holistically, in a closely integrated manner, to serve clients effectively. Your level of benefits is linked to your retirement account, both of which affect the amount of life insurance you can afford, which impacts your personal investment strategy…

Needless to say, the old Org Chart was useless at capturing this complexity. Smith is a well-run business, but leaders had no clear way to represent its complicated functions and structure. We introduced the Organizational Cognizance Model and helped the organization to complete the Cracking Eggs and Flower Power exercises from the previous chapter, and to build an Org Graph.

Once the Org Graph was installed, the organization lit up. Everyone knew who was doing what and how he or she related to colleagues and Processes across the company. They understood how their work affected others, how various functions were coordinated, the Purpose behind formerly murky Procedures/Work Inst./Policies and Systems. The number of questions ICs had dwindled because the Org Graph itself answered many of them. It was as if people had been working by candlelight, and someone switched the lights on.

The Organizational Cognizance we achieved with Smith also led to better and more coordinated service for customers. In this case, Smith showed its Org Graph to clients to educate them on how they would be served and how the organization conducted this very complicated business.

For most businesses, the Org Graph is strictly internal, but Smith used it as a way to win business, as well as to help existing clients navigate its services.

Example 2: A project-based marketing company creating templates.

Another organization that we are working with also completed our Organizational Cognizance exercises and installed an Org Graph but with a very different approach that grew organically from its business. This company, which we will call College Marketing, handles marketing for universities, everything from websites and social media to ad campaigns and promotional pieces.

We built College Marketing's Org Graph around its primary Workflow for a university client that wants the full menu of services. All of the Nodes and Edges involved in that Workflow – Jobs, Roles, Objectives, Meetings, Procedures/Work Inst./Policies, etc. – form a template: here is how we serve a client who wants our full offerings, soup to nuts, front to back. When this kind of client hires the organization, College Marketing turns to an unpopulated Org Graph template that covers everything and then attaches People to the new project via Job and Role Edges.

For a la carte clients, or those who want a particular set of services, parts of the overall Org Graph template can be utilized, brought to the forefront, and others left dormant. With a few mouse clicks, we can say, okay, here is the Workflow for the soup course only – with all its attendant Jobs, Roles, Objectives, humans to do the work, etc. – if that's what the client wants. For a client who wants three of eight courses, we can activate those parts of the overall Graph. We turn to the appropriate parts of an unpopulated template and then pull in Bob, Kim, and Alice, who are assigned the appropriate Roles. They instantly know what Objectives they're **AccountableFor**, the Results they're **ResponsibleFor**, the Meetings they'll **Attend**, the Systems they'll **InterfaceWith**, etc. to serve this client. They understand their Purpose, domain, and authority – and that their Roles can shift from client to client, or project to project on a fairly routine basis.

The usual setup time and throat-clearing that occurs before work on a project really begins is eliminated. Bob, Kim, and Alice can plunge right in, fully Cognizant, and they're less likely to suffer missteps or confusion, since the roadmap to serve this particular client with this set of needs is crystal clear.

SELF-INTEGRATING TEAMS

Because of the limitations of space and print, we are barely scratching the surface of how Organizational Cognizance and the Org Graph can benefit organizations. As we hope you see from the examples above, the Org Graph is as flexible and nimble as your business. It gets built according to the needs, priorities, and quirks of a particular organization. The overall principles and component parts are the same, but the Org Graphs for Smith Planning and University Marketing are quite different. Both organizations accelerated onboarding and employee ROI with their Org Graphs and created a new level of transparency, but as we've seen, they also use their Graphs in unique ways.

This is another benefit of a 3-D Org Graph updated in real time – it is tailored to your evolving organization on a daily – really, minute-by-minute – basis. The old Org Chart, by contrast, looks more or less the same all year and from business to business – a vague pyramid that doesn't tell anyone much about the reality of how your organization works or how ICs are actually connected.

In previous chapters, we discussed how having an IC start a new Job with an Org Graph that visualizes exactly where she fits and how things function – every Meeting, System, Procedures/Work Inst./Policies, and Workflow she touches – creates clarity, engagement, and buy-in. We have talked about how it boosts performance and answers the questions that ICs are often afraid to ask. We have talked about the ways that the Org Graph accelerates onboarding, and at the end of Chapter 1, we did the math showing that, minimally, the Organizational Cognizance Model and Org Graph can produce a permanent 15 percent gain in employee productivity. That's a dividend paid directly to your EBITDA – and it's a conservative estimate.

These are the benefits for a single IC and those who work with him or her, as well as for the organization. Once every Job and Role is accurately represented in a 3-D Org Graph, however, the benefits multiply exponentially. Everyone's level of awareness, knowledge, and connectedness reaches new heights. People understand their own Jobs and Roles with new clarity, but also the Jobs and Roles of everyone they work with or are linked to.

As the Org Graph fills out, Teams also understand other Teams, and Departments other Departments at a deeper level. Organizations that achieve Cognizance develop what we call self-integrating Teams. Everyone on the Team is Cognizant of how and where they fit. They are hyperaware of that domed-top table from our earlier illustration and the role their Roles play in making sure nothing slips through the cracks. They fully understand their domain and authority, which prevents the jockeying that occurs within and between teams – and almost always results from a lack of clarity.

We are not saying there will never be an ego that needs to be checked or an IC with a propensity for wandering out of his lane. We are saying that with an Org Graph in place and a functioning Organizational Cognizance Model installed, the self-integrated Team will usually take care of these issues itself because Accountability and connections are now clear. Bob and Kim, from our College Marketing example above, will quickly spot what's slipping through the cracks and trace it back to Alice with the help of their updated Org Graph. With that Org Graph in hand – or rather, on screen –

they'll feel comfortable going over her Roles with her, pointing out a Procedures/Work Inst./Policy she's skipping or Key Results she's missing, in a way that they wouldn't without that clear visualization of *who is doing what.*

In his acclaimed book, *The Five Dysfunctions of a Team,* Patrick Lencioni argues that avoiding the Responsibility of calling out peers who are falling short is one of the primary problems Teams face. It's a problem that largely disappears when true Accountability is built into an Org Graph.

We have used the word "Accountability" a lot, though we acknowledge that in some ways, it's a tired term. What leaders really think when they utter this word is a useful acronym, DYFJ: Do Your Fricking Job. That's the bottom-line, isn't it? Well, it's much easier to DYFJ if you are Cognizant of what that Job is. And it's easier still when everyone on your Team also understands what it is, right down to every Role that is a **FunctionOf** your Job, every Meeting you **Attend**, and Key Result you're **ResponsibleFor**. If something slips through the cracks or someone oversteps his domain or authority, fellow Team members are now much more likely to reach over for a course correction because they know where the lines are.

As we saw in Chapter 2, research demonstrates that the move from hierarchical to more Team-centric models can improve performance, but the Deloitte survey we cited reveals that only 6 percent of respondents rate themselves as "very effective" at managing cross-functional Teams. The growth of Teams is a sign that organizational structures have evolved in the face of 21st-century technology and challenges. The classic Org Chart has not, and therein lies the troubling gap that led to the Org Graph.

SELF-ACCOUNTABILITY IS THE ONLY KIND

We want to return to the term "Accountability" and expand on why we use it with some uneasiness. It gets bandied about in business all the time.

> *Hold your people Accountable,* we hear. *Why aren't you holding him Accountable for these numbers? I'm going to hold the entire team Accountable for making this deadline…*

We said early in Chapter 1 that this book grew as we focused on the difficult "hinge" of the Seven Questions critical to cultivating engaged team members, detailed in my previous book, *The Patient Organization*. We phrased this hinge question "Am I Accountable?" and we have returned again and again to Accountability. It is at the heart of the Org Graph and the Organizational Cognizance Model.

"Accountability" is central to everything here, but the word gets used in misleading ways. At 7Q7P, we believe deeply that you cannot *hold* someone Accountable in an organization. The only three people who can hold me Accountable are me, myself, and I. Rather than saying, *you need to hold Fred Accountable*, we believe, the smarter stance is, *how can we create the awareness – better yet, Cognizance – that will allow Fred to hold himself Accountable?*

The common usage, *holding* people Accountable, arises from an old hierarchical, command-and-control approach. *Hold* someone Accountable? Think about that language. Sounds more appropriate for a wrestling match or a prison than a 21st-century business, right? The phrase and the philosophy behind it reflect the rigid old Org Chart, a schematic designed for layers of workers to be controlled by ever-smaller layers as we work our way up a food chain. It was fine back in the old nine-to-five days when everyone reported to one brick-and-mortar office and had a single boss. It was fine when thinking was done at the top by a few lieutenants and the formula *Person = Job* held true. In an era of fluid Teams, project-based work, diffuse thinking, telecommuting, mobile offices, automation, and globalization, it is no longer fine.

We hear "Accountable" and think, *supervision, oppression, management, leash*. We are trying to take the word back with the Org Graph and the Organizational Cognizance Model, where Accountability isn't oppressive but liberating. The old-school notion that ICs must be "managed" because their default is to avoid Accountability is, excuse my French, B.S. ICs want to be led, not managed, and they want *real* Accountability more than anything. The Gallup numbers we saw in Chapter 1, indicating that more than two-thirds of U.S. workers are not actively engaged, result largely from ICs' deep-seated frustration that leaders are not communicating clearly or creating the conditions for true Accountability, i.e. *Self*-Accountability.

We explore this concept in depth in *The Patient Organization,* where we argue that real Accountability – which requires understanding clearly the Objectives and Key Results you're aiming for and all of the moving parts that get you to them – can turn drones into stars. It can transform frustrated ICs into engaged problem-solvers by opening clear communication channels, establishing fair and transparent measures, setting concrete goals, and putting ICs in control of their own work.

The million-dollar challenge is how to achieve this kind of Accountability. The solution is the Org Graph and the Organizational Cognizance Method. As we've mentioned, this book and the Org Graph grew out of the need for concrete strategies to get to *yes* to that critical hinge, Question three: *Am I Accountable?* The Org Graph offers ICs real Accountability by revealing with just a couple of mouse clicks exactly where they fit in the organization. With the Org Graph, they know with utter clarity what Objectives they are **AccountableFor** and the Key Results they are **ResponsibleFor** achieving – Nodes and Edges that they themselves create. They can see exactly what Meetings they'll **Attend**, the Workflow they'll **ParticipateIn**, the Procedures/Work Inst./Policies they'll **Follow**, and the Systems they'll **InterfaceWith** in order to meet those Objectives and Key Results. With input from leaders, they build and update the Org Graph themselves, and they are Accountable in the truest sense – to themselves.

In those rare instances when an IC is constitutionally averse to work, with an Org Graph in place, there's nowhere to hide. There's no way to claim you didn't know what you were **ResponsibleFor** or **AccountableFor**, the Procedures/Work Inst./Policies you should have **Followed**, the Mentor you might have asked for help, or the Entities you needed to **InteractWith**. It's all right there on screen, controlled by you, with input from a leader and available in multiple helpful views. If the problem is a lack of Skills, that's also evident on the Org Graph, in the gap between "**Has**" and "**Requires**" on the Skills Node.

ANSWERING THE 7 QUESTIONS

As we helped clients that we were coaching install the Org Graph in our first test runs, we could see – and they agreed – that it created true Accountability better than any other tool in our arsenal. The Org graph does more than that, however. The drive to create the Org Graph began with the third of the Seven Questions vital for engagement, but it actually helps organizations get to *yes* on all of them.

To review, our work coaching organizations over the years (more than 200 by the time of this writing, big and small, in many fields) led us to the Seven Questions and Seven Promises critical to cultivating culture and engaged team members. These are *the* seven critical things that ICs want to say *yes* to and the seven fundamental Promises that a Cognizant organization must make:

The individual must say *yes* absolutely	The organization must say *yes* absolutely
1. **Do I belong?** (I fit the organization's core values and have the skill needed for my Job and Roles). **I Belong.**	1. We have clearly defined our core values and the skills necessary for every *Job* and *Role* are clearly laid out.
2. **Do I believe?** (I am motivated by the mission and the strategic direction leadership is taking). **I Believe.**	2. We know our *Why, our Focus,* and have a clearly mapped out strategy with priorities determined, laid out and shared.
3. **Am I Accountable?** (I understand and embrace the Purpose of my Job and Roles, what I should be thinking and doing). **Yes, I am Accountable.**	3. Our Accountability and Responsibility structure is clear. See the Organizational Cognizance Model 14 Point Checklist.
4. **Am I measured well?** (I understand and embrace how and why I am measured, I know what a good job is and agree with the metrics). **Yes, I understand and embrace how I am Measured.**	4. We have metrics, Objectives and Key Results for team members that inform them, giving them the latitude to form strategies to achieve these OKRs.
5. **Is my opinion is heard?** (I understand and embrace how my organization listens and how I my opinion is heard.) **Yes, I understand and embrace how I am heard.**	5. We have clearly mapped out and defined the communication channels we use to listen and communicate – our meetings, mentoring, etc. – build trust, spur debate and help our ICs grow.
6. **Am I being developed?** (I understand and embrace how my organization offers	6. We have clearly mapped out systematic development pathways for

opportunities for development and I take an active role in my own development) **Yes, I understand and embrace how I am developed.**	employees to participate in for their own development. This includes a combination of On-The-Job training, formal training, mentoring, coaching and accountability.
7. Do I have balance? (I understand and embrace what the organization's definition of balance is from a work-life, health and compensation perspective.) **Yes, I understand and embrace how my balance is maintained.**	7. We have taken the time to clearly define and communicate what work-life balance is to this organization and have communicated it up front with everyone. We have clear paths for employees to follow to maintain health and wellness balance and our compensation structures are clear and out in the open for the ICs to consider.

If ICs can answer *yes* to all of these, you have Organizational Cognizance. The Org Graph, along with our Organizational Cognizance exercises, the Organizational Graph Worksheet, etc. are vital tools for getting there. We have already addressed the many ways that the Org Graph elicits a *yes* on the hinge question, "Am I Accountable?" How does it help with the others?

ADDRESSING THE 7 QUESTIONS AND 7 PROMISES THROUGH THE ORGANIZATIONAL COGNIZANCE LENS

1. Do I belong?

Questions one and two are the most foundational. If you've seen our Org Graph screenshots throughout the book, it should be apparent how the Organizational Cognizance Model helps answer the first of these, "Do I belong?" The IC can see on the Org Graph exactly what Skills her job **Requires**, as well as those Required for each of the Job's Roles. That's one arrow, or Edge, coming off our Skills Node. A second Edge, pointing in the other direction, shows what Skills the Person **Has**. If there are areas where the IC is falling short – the gap between what's Required and what she Has – they're easy to spot and work on. In a larger sense, seeing every connection the IC has – to colleagues, supervisors, Teams, Meetings, Processes, Procedures/Work Inst./Policies, etc. – demonstrates exactly where she fits, or belongs, and how this organization runs. If she can't get on board with this structure or doesn't like her place in it, determining that she doesn't belong should be a quick process, which saves grief for both her and the organization. The other side of the "belong" coin is the core values fit, covered deeply in *The Patient Organization.*

2. **Do I believe?**

We have talked in depth about belief. This question is existential, since as I've said, an organization is really just a fiction, recreated every day by the ICs who believe in it. The main barrier to this all-important belief is ignorance. People simply don't know, because they haven't been told, what it is that they're supposed to believe in. Poor communication can result in twenty people believing one thing, thirty another, and the remaining fifty yet another – in which case, you have three organizations, not one. The Org Graph lays out in the most concrete terms what you are being asked to believe in – from the overall organizational mission down to every last Workflow, Procedures/Work Inst./Policy, and Meeting. The organization's CEO has a Purpose Statement in the Organizational Cognizance model, in the perfect world, an IC can access and read the CEO's Purpose Statements and can see her Objectives creating clarity, openness and Cognizance. Equally important, though absent from other models, Purpose Statements are written by ICs for every Role they own. As a result, they are Cognizant of the *why, how,* and *what* – to borrow Simon Sinek's schema – from the macro view down to the micro. As I said in Chapter 1, belief demands Cognizance.

3. **Am I Accountable?**

We covered this thoroughly above. To recap, Self-Accountability – the only true kind – requires understanding clearly the Objectives and Key Results you're aiming for and all of the moving parts that get you to them – the Meetings, Processes, Procedures/Work Inst./Policies, Systems, Entities, etc. The Org Graph brings a new level of transparency to all of these Nodes and Edges, putting ICs in control of their own work and performance.

4. **Am I measured well?**

The specifics of this Question vary from industry to industry, and I explore how to establish solid fair measures in depth in *The Patient*

Organization. The common complaint about metrics across industries, though, is that they often seem unfair, leaving ICs feeling as if they've been set up to fail. By clearly detailing the Purpose, Objectives, and Key Results not just for every Job but for every Role that's a **FunctionOf** a Job, the Org Graph makes ICs Cognizant of just how they will be measured from day one. Links to documents and webpages related to specific measures can be embedded right in the Objectives and Key Results Nodes for each Role, as can Rich-Text explanations of metrics. Further, the Graph demonstrates exactly who will Coach an IC for each Role and offer guidance as challenges arise. Because all Nodes and Edges are spelled out and the IC knows exactly where she fits, she understands that she is being measured within a system she fully grasps. Without the clarity of an Org Graph, the same IC at a typical organization can feel as if she's being graded on how well she navigates a maze with blinders on. We suggest a one-on-one Seasonal Meeting (explored thoroughly in *TPO*), which we'll talk about in our section on maintenance below, as a built-in opportunity to warn ICs if they're falling short on metrics and to hear their opinions if measures seem flawed.

5. **Is my opinion heard?**

   All communication channels are also spelled out in the Org Graph, from the Coach an IC turns to about the details of each Role to the Systems she **InterfacesWith** (including CRM software, project platforms, etc.) to the Meetings where she can express concerns, comments, and questions. The Org Graph reflects these channels, and is itself one of the chief ways that individuals are heard. The Cracking Eggs and Flower Power exercises and the Organizational Cognizance Role Capture Worksheet are a chance for everyone in the organization to talk about their Purpose, Roles, domain, authority, and capacity. From the CEO to the newest frontline IC, everyone maintains Nodes and Edges, informing everyone what his Job is, what he does, why, and how. Here, too, the one-on-one Seasonal Meeting is vital. It is a formal, programmed space set aside four times a year for ICs to meet with a Mentor and discuss, with the help of the Org Graph, their place within the organization, their goals, obstacles, performance, concerns about Roles and other Nodes, etc.

6. **Am I being developed?**

One way that the Org Graph helps ICs answer yes to this question is simply by spelling out the Mentors offering guidance on career paths. Big deal, you say? Well, yes, it actually is, especially since this connection is not on the old Org Chart (an IC's boss frequently is not his or her Mentor) and is often not communicated effectively by organizations. Yes, being clear and current about this connection, or Edge, is a simple, painless way to boost engagement, lower turnover, and improve performance by highlighting an IC's future within the organization. Why then do I encounter so many companies with no mechanism for making this clear and for keeping the connection up-to-date? The Org Graph makes **MentoredBy** one of the primary Edges, signaling that an IC's future is as important to the organization as Objectives and Key Results. There are many other ways that the Org Graph helps ICs answer *yes* to this Question, but in the interests of space, I'll just give a couple more examples. An IC who wants to move forward into a new Job within an organization can easily pull it up on the Org Graph, check out the Skills it **Requires**, and then compare that Node to her own Skills Node. She now knows what she must work on to advance to the new Job. From another angle, let's say an Account Manager at an organization starts out at Level 1, then can move up to Account Manager 2, Account Manager 3, etc. The key difference is that an Account Manager 1 handles four Roles, an Account Manager 2 handles six, an Account Manager 3 handles eight, and so on. An Account Manager who wants to move up to the next level has a built-in roadmap for how to get there in the Org Graph, where the Roles that are a **FunctionOf** each job are listed.

7. **Do I have balance?**

The work that allows you to say *yes* to having a good work-life balance rests mostly with the IC. The Organizational Cognizance Model helps Individual Contributors here through our Flower Power exercise before they even fill out their Nodes on the Org Graph. As ICs in similar jobs do this exercise together (refer back to Chapter 3 if you need a refresher), issues of capacity will come to light. If things are slipping through the cracks, is it because a particular IC doesn't understand his Roles, or doesn't want to succeed in them, or doesn't have the capacity for his current workload? The exhaustive inventory we do in this exercise often reveals structural problems affecting work-life balance and points to adjustments that get it back on track. Once the Org Graph is filled out, it also has the power to quickly and clearly illustrate the pressure points preventing a *yes* on balance. Frequently, a deeply engaged IC steps forward to pick up the slack when someone is let go, for example. In this case, a Role (sometimes several) gets linked to his Job on the Org Graph. That temporary fill-in can become a permanent burden, burning out a motivated IC who's being forced to operate outside his or her domain and authority. The Org Graph acts as a check against this imbalance by highlighting temporary Roles (they can even be color-coded according to how urgently they need to be handed off as new ICs are hired). Similarly, old Roles that should be given up as an IC takes on new ones when he or she advances into a new Job have a tendency to linger. The Org Graph highlights the sticky Roles that upset work-life balance and need to go.

MAINTAINING COGNIZANCE

We will close *Death of the Org Chart* with a discussion of how to maintain Organizational Cognizance. My sincere hope, though, is that this is not a conclusion for you but the beginning of a long and fruitful journey. The "death" of the Org Chart spells the birth of the Org Graph, which will grow and evolve with your organization. It is not a one-and-done affair, any more than planting a garden is. Without pruning, weeding, and fertilizing, a garden quickly reverts to jungle, and organizations are no different.

The Org Graph must be continually updated, reviewed, and maintained, but the good news is that it is largely self-maintaining and self-correcting. As We've said, ICs participate in building their own Nodes and Edges in the Organizational Cognizance Model, and our Organizational Graph software is designed with this sort of self-maintenance in mind. Anyone who's ever used a computer can begin clicking on icons to create their Nodes and Edges immediately. With the help of a supervisor, a new IC can begin updating or building Nodes for Roles, Objectives, Key Results, Systems, Workflow, Procedures/Work Inst./Policies, Meetings, etc. his or her first week.

Having ICs help build, maintain, and update the Org Graph familiarizes them with the tool, educates them about their Roles and other Nodes, and keeps them focused on their Objectives and Key Results. For Organizational Cognizance to take hold, we want ICs referencing the Org Graph on a regular basis as they reflect on the agenda of an upcoming Meeting, the Purpose of a Procedures/Work Inst./Policy that's part of their Workflow, the Mentor they can ask about a new challenge…We want them to see in this clear visualization where they fit within the organization, how they are connected to other ICs, Teams, and Processes.

We want them to know *who is doing what and why*, and *what am I doing and why*.

Having ICs maintain the Org Graph themselves – with input from leaders, of course – boosts what we have been calling *Self*-Accountability. Having Objectives and Key Results hammered into you helter-skelter by a boss, or several, is one thing. Helping to create them yourself in a clear visualization that connects them to all the moving parts you touch, with the ability to view it through a variety of helpful lenses, is quite another. The second option puts the IC in control of her work, results, and advancement. It gives her ownership and allows her to answer *yes* to the vital hinge question of the big Seven: *Do I understand and embrace what I am Accountable for?* As we've seen, it also helps get her to *yes* on the other six Questions too.

This is why all ICs, whatever their Jobs and Roles, have one Role in common, the one we label "Org Graph Maintenance" in the Organizational Cognizance Model. Keeping your piece of the Org Graph accurate and up-to-date, with all Edges spelled out, all Meetings accounted for, new Systems added, dated Procedures revised, etc. is a part of every single Job. Making Maintenance a formal Role, and not just something that's mentioned as an administrative chore, emphasizes the importance of the Org Graph for ICs and keeps them focused on the tool that will help them reach Cognizance.

It's the grease that keeps the machinery working and a check against the dysfunction that's the opposite of Cognizance.

THE SEASONAL MEETING

Another key tool that maintains Cognizance is the one-on-one Seasonal Meeting, which we touched on above and write about extensively in *The Patient Organization.* We recommend that you read that book for best practices around this opportunity to affirm a *yes* to each of the Seven Questions and to formally review each IC's place in the Org Graph.

The general idea is that every IC should be meeting with a Coach (supervisor, Team leader, Mentor, etc.) every ninety days. The overall agenda for this meeting is the Org Graph and the Seven Questions. Since the Organizational Cognizance Model is built on Self-Accountability, with ICs creating their own portions of the Org Graph and answering the Seven Questions themselves, the IC leads the meeting.

The IC should review and evaluate the Key Results she is **ResponsibleFor** and the Objectives she is **AccountableFor**, using the Org Graph and whatever metrics the organization has established (creating solid metrics is also covered in depth in *The Patient Organization).* How does she evaluate her own performance? What areas need improvement? What Skills does she want or need to work on? How is she being developed?

It is as easy as going down the 14 Point Cognizance Checklist.

Reviewing the Org Graph together, the IC and Coach can also make any necessary adjustments at the Seasonal Meeting. There shouldn't be much to adjust, since the Org Graph is continually updated, but this a formal chance to affirm that it's being well maintained and reflects the reality of the IC's organizational life (unlike the static Org Chart).

Do any new Roles need to be connected to her Job or old ones cut or shifted on the Org Graph? Are her Roles capturing everything they need to, with no items slipping in between (remember the dome-topped table)? Is her capacity at the right level – Roles not so full that items are spilling over and not so empty that she isn't challenged and engaged? Is every Meeting this

IC Attends on the Graph? Is every System she **InterfacesWith** accounted for? Is she still **InteractingWith** all of the Entities listed as connections to her Roles?

The Seasonal Meeting is a chance to look ahead and plan, too. How should Objectives be adjusted for the next season? What Key Results will help the IC achieve them? What Skills might she work on (including certifications, classes, trainings) to make sure that she belongs (Question 1) and is developed (Question 6)? If her work-life balance (Question 7) is out of whack, what will she do to recalibrate?

The Seasonal Meeting is led by and focused on the IC, but as you walk through his or her portion of the Org Graph, the process inevitably leads to discoveries that affect the whole organization (Organizational Cognizance is all about a deep awareness of how Nodes are connected). Bottlenecks in a Workflow will come to light, Roles that are redundant, Meetings that have grown too large or lost focus. With a heightened sense of control and Self-Accountability, the IC is often the one to see and raise such problems.

CRACK SOME MORE EGGS, WATER YOUR FLOWERS

Like the Seasonal Meeting, our key Organizational Cognizance exercises, Cracking Eggs and Flower Power, and the Organizational Cognizance Role Capture Worksheets, must be revisited periodically to keep the Org Graph up to date and to maintain Cognizance. Whenever fuzziness arises about who is Accountable for what or people begin complaining about a lack of capacity or a Team says, sorry, we just don't have the bandwidth to get that done, it's time to get people in a room and take a full inventory of what everyone is doing.

The A-players who pick up slack or fill in when someone leaves or there's a rush of new business, tend to hang onto those sticky Roles, no matter how temporary they are supposed to be. The Org Graph makes such problems of capacity, domain, and authority easy to spot, and a new round of Cracking Eggs and Flower Power allow the organization to make the necessary adjustments to Roles and Jobs.

If you repeat the Organizational Cognizance exercises as needed, schedule Seasonal Meetings every ninety days, and most important, make Org Graph Maintenance a standard Role for every IC, your Graph will remain current, vital, and eminently useful. The organization will build and maintain Cognizance because it's now part and parcel of your culture. It will be understood that new ICs hit the ground running. They start work aware of the Processes they **ParticipateIn**, the Procedures/Work Inst./Policies they **Follow**, the Systems they **InterfaceWith**, and the Teams they are **MembersOf**. Every IC appreciates why each Meeting he Attends is important, and how it relates to his Roles and Purpose. All systems – ERP, HRIS, accounting, Supply Chain, Facilities, etc. – are fully integrated, with connections clearly spelled out, and our Teams largely run themselves because this is who we are.

New ICs stepping into a Job will have a deep well of organizational knowledge to draw on, and their onboarding will be faster and easier. They will be more engaged, and you will experience less turnover. They will perform better and bring a faster ROI – all of which has a positive effect on the bottom line.

These benefits are obvious, but the Org Graph brings others that are tougher to quantify. ICs will experience an atmosphere where people know at a deep level what's going on. They'll understand where they fit within the organization, how their work affects others, *who is doing what,* and why – and they'll be surrounded by people with this same deep level of understanding. With the Org Graph and the Organizational Cognizance Model in place, you will have what we think of as a Culture of Cognizance. In such a culture, leaders can *lead*, rather than simply manage, and engaged ICs can enjoy true Accountability. An organization with this sort of culture, with real Cognizance, has everything it needs to leave the competition in the dust.

CONCLUSION: WELCOME TO REALITY

Death of the Org Chart is designed to be an introduction. It is necessarily brief and abridged because, unfortunately, the paper product in your hand has the same limitations as another two-dimensional artifact, the old Org Chart. We have printed screenshots throughout the book, and we'll include more in an appendix. We've printed and defined the Nodes and Edges used in our Org Graph software, and we've explained the Org Graph and Organizational Cognizance Model as best we can, but none of this is adequate.

If a picture is worth a thousand words, a few minutes experiencing an actual Org Graph online is worth 20,000. We encourage you to go to https://ograph.io where you can watch a couple of short demos that display an Org Graph in action. They'll show you much better than we can here how useful an Org Graph can be and how simple it is to begin building one of your own.

At https://ograph.io you can test various features and take the software for a spin to try out our tool for building an Org Graph. As we've said, our Graph Database software is by no means mandatory. If you have another way to visualize organizational complexity this clearly in a user-friendly format with multiple views, you can use it to create your Org Graph. This is simply the best solution we've found, a tailor-made answer to the inadequacies of the classic Org Chart that we've been struggling with for years. Whatever means you choose to build your Org Graph, we recommend that you start with the visualizations at https://ograph.io simply to see how an actual Org Graph looks and functions.

To learn more about the Seven Questions and Seven Promises critical to cultivating culture and engaged ICs – only lightly touched on here – we recommend that you read *The Patient Organization*. That earlier book provides the philosophical and psychological underpinnings of the Organizational Cognizance Model, a deep-dive on each of the Seven Questions, and concrete strategies and exercises – the "Heavy Lifts" – that get you to *yes* and foster Organizational Cognizance. You can learn more about *The Patient Organization,* as well as the Seven Questions and Seven

Promises Momentum framework at www.7q7p.com and at https://sevenpromises.university

The fact that you're holding this book means that you get it. You have understood, maybe for a long time, that using the old Org Chart feels like making complex calculations on an abacus instead of a computer. You have known that a better tool was needed, one that reflects the messy reality of a complicated 21st century organization, but until now, none was available. Embracing this new tool as an early adopter will give you a significant edge over the competition.

Congratulations and welcome to the 21st century. You have taken the Red Pill, to return to our *Matrix* analogy, and are well on your way to answering Peter Drucker's all-important question, *who is doing what?* You are on the road to Organizational Cognizance.

The Org Chart is dead. Long live the Org Graph!

Stay patient, my friends.

Love,

Walt

APPENDIX

Four Flower Power Board Examples

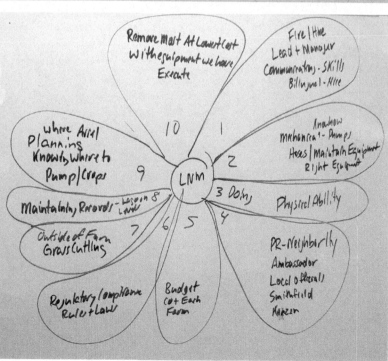

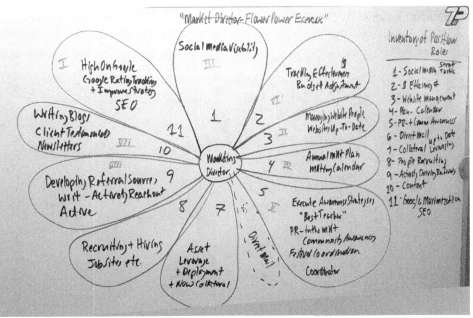

"Market Director Flower Power Exercise"

Marketing Director (center)

Inventory of Position Roles
1 - Social Media — Strat Tactic
2 - $ Efficiency #
3 - Website management
4 - Plan - Calendar
5 - PR + Comm Awareness
6 - Direct Mail up to Date
7 - Collateral Leverage
8 - People Recruiting
9 - Actively Driving Referrals
10 - Content
11 - Google Maximization SEO

- High On Google, Google Rating Tracking + Improve Strategy SEO
- Social Media Visibility
- Tracking Effectiveness Budget Adjustment
- Writing Blogs, Client Testimonials, Newsletters
- Managing Website People, Website Up-To-Date
- Annual Mrkt Plan, Marketing Calendar
- Developing Referral Sources, Writ - Actively Reach out Active
- Execute Awareness Strategy "Best Teacher", PR - in the mrkt Community Awareness, Festival Coordination Coordinator
- Recruiting + Hiring, Jobsites etc.
- Asset Leverage + Deployment + New Collateral
- Direct Mail

LMA   Internship   Hiring Recruiting
               RP/RS   Mentor/Trainer

Biz Special Projects   1   2

12   3   P/L - Profit 1st
                                   Scorecards #

Capacity Police   Integrator   4   Detail/
Logic/Throttle/Scale   Remove Daily
                                     Obstacle

O'Graph   5   Listen late to John's
Workflows Create 10   Ideas
Process/Docu   "Same Day/month"
Enforce/Improve   Stay In Lane

           8   6   EOS/7Q/OCM SSS/L10
                        #s Goals
Acquisition/m'A   7   ERP/Desco
Integration   Parts/Inventory
       Drive Mrktg
       Sales
       Sales Mindset
       Branding
       Cost Retention

ORGANIZATIONAL COGNIZANCE™

A Chart - OCOG - Seat and Roles - 15 Point Cognizance Model

EOS® Accountability Chart
[Structure First | People Second]

Each Seat has a well written purpose statement.

Seats

Each Role has a well written purpose statement.

Roles

A Person Owns a Seat - Roles to Seats

Seats Report To Seats

EOS® Accountability Chart Extended
with OCOG 15 Pt Cognizance Model

1. Seats with Purpose Statements
2. Roles with Purpose Statements
3. Reports To

4. + Teams - *Member Of*
5. + Meetings - *Attends*
6. + Entities - *Interacts With*
7. + Objectives - *Accountable For*
8. + Key Results - *Responsible For*
9. + Processes - *Participates In*
10. + Procedures, Work Inst., Policies - *Followed*
11. + Systems - *Interface With*
12. + Skills - *Required, Have*
13. + Coached By
14. + Mentored By
15. + Department

= Cognizance

Captured and visualized with Graph Database software.

Extending your Roles to the other 14 Points Matrix worksheet.

OCOG - Seat and Roles 15 Point Matrix Worksheet

Fill in Row >	Primary Seat	Role 1	Role 2	Role 3	Role 4	Role 5	Role etc.
Seat	Primary Seat						
Report To							
Teams							
Meetings							
Entities							
Objectives							
Key Results							
Processes							
Procedures / WIs / Policies							
Systems							
Skills							
Department							
Coached By							
Mentored By							

ORGANIZATIONAL COGNIZANCE®

EOS® Accountability Chart
[Structure First | People Second]

Seats

Each Seat has a well written purpose statement.

Roles

Each Role has a well written purpose statement.

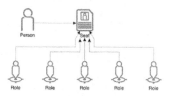

A Person Owns a Seat - Roles to Seats

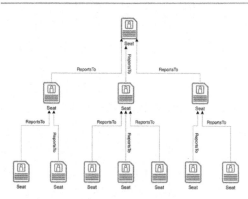

Seats Report To Seats

Using ograph.io to visualize the basic Roles and Reporting work from the EOS® Accountability Chart.

Basic elements and Nodes of Jobs and Roles.

Job	Element/Node	Role
•	Purpose Statement	•
•	Objective	•
•	Key Result	•
•	Skills	•
•	Systems	•
•	Procedures/Work Inst./Policies	•
•	Processes	•
•	Teams	•
•	Meetings	•
•	Entities	•
ReportsTo		**FunctionOf**
MentoredBy		**CoachedBy**

Basic Organizational Cognizance Graph Database Model

Extended List of all Edges and the Nodes they connect.

Source Node	Edge	Target Node
Role	**CoachedBy**	Role
Role	**FunctionOf**	Job
Role	**AccountableFor**	Objective
Role	**ResponsibleFor**	Result
Role	**Attends**	Meeting
Role	**MemberOf**	Team
Role	**ParticipatesIn**	Workflow
Role	**Follows**	Procedures/Work Inst./Policy
Role	**Maintains**	Procedures/Work Inst./Policy
Role	**InterfacesWith**	System
Role	**InteractsWith**	Entity
Role	**ContributesTo**	Objective

Role	Requires	Skill
Job	**AccountableFor**	Objective
Job	**ResponsibleFor**	Result
Job	**Attends**	Meeting
Job	**MemberOf**	Team
Job	**ParticipatesIn**	Workflow
Job	**Follows**	Procedures/Work Inst./Policy
Job	**Maintains**	Procedures/Work Inst./Policy
Job	**InterfacesWith**	System
Job	**InteractsWith**	Entity
Job	**ContributesTo**	Objective
Job	**MentoredBy**	Job
Job	**ReportsTo**	Job
Job	**Requires**	Skill
Person	**Owns**	Job
Person	**Has**	Skill
Procedures/Work Inst./Policy	**Procedures/Work Inst./Policy Of**	Workflow
Objective	**Supports**	Objective
Result	**Enables**	Objective
Workflow	**Sub**	Workflow
Entity	**BelongsTo**	Entity

Additional Resources:

"The Patient Organization" is a companion book to popular Organizational Operating Systems like EOS™ (aka Traction™) and Scaling Up™ etc. and is meant to add momentum to your efforts.

The Patient Organization   Walt Brown

https://deathoftheorgchart.com

https://thepatientorganization.com

https://sevenpromises.university

https://7q7p.com

https://organizationalcognizance.university

https://ocog.io

https://ograph.io

We hold workshop events either virtually or in person in Chapel Hill NC. Learn about these offerings at https://organizationalcognizance.university

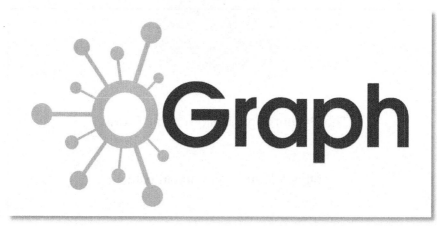

In addition to Death we have a software solution https://ograph.io that uses graph database technology to capture and visualize the rubrics discussed throughout The Patient Organization and expanded in Death of the Org Chart.

Made in the USA
Middletown, DE
21 April 2022

64590935R00066